Table of Contents

Taking Standardized Tests

No matter what grade you're in, this is information you can use to prepare for standardized tests. Here is what you'll find:

- Test-taking tips and strategies to use on test day and year round.
- Important terms to know for Language Arts, Reading, Math, Science, and Social Studies.
- A checklist of skills to complete to help you understand what you need to know in Language Arts, Reading Comprehension, Writing, and Math.
- General study/homework tips.

By opening this book, you've already taken your first step towards test success. The rest is easy—all you have to do is get started!

What You Need to Know

There are many things you can do to increase your test success. Here's a list of tips to keep in mind when you take standardized tests—and when you study for them, too.

Keep up with your school work. One way you can succeed in school and on tests is by studying and doing your homework regularly. Studies show that you remember only about one-fifth of what you memorize the night before a test. That's one good reason not to try to learn it all at once! Keeping up with your work throughout the year will help you remember the material better. You also won't be as tired or nervous as if you try to learn everything at once.

Feel your best. One of the ways you can

do your best on tests and in school is to make sure your body is ready. To do this, get a good night's sleep each night and eat a healthy breakfast (not sugary cereal that will leave you tired by the middle of the morning). An egg or a milkshake with yogurt and fresh fruit will give you lasting energy. Also, wear comfortable clothes, maybe your lucky shirt or your favorite color on test day. It can't hurt, and it may even help you relax.

Be prepared. Do practice questions and learn about how standardized tests are organized. Books like this one will help you know what to expect when you take a standardized test.

When you are taking the test, follow the directions. It is important to listen carefully to the directions your teacher gives and to read the written instructions carefully. Words like *not, none, rarely, never,* and *always* are very important in test directions and questions. You may want to circle words like these.

Look at each page carefully before you start answering. In school you usually read a passage and then answer questions about it. But when you take a test, it's helpful to follow a different order.

If you are taking a Reading test, first read the directions. Then read the questions before you read the passage. This way, you will know exactly what kind of information to look for as you read. Next, read the passage carefully. Finally, answer the questions.

On math and science tests, look at the labels on graphs and charts. Think about what each graph or chart shows. Questions often will ask you to draw conclusions about the information.

Manage your time. *Time management* means using your time wisely on a test so that you can finish as much of it as possible and do your best. Look over the test or the parts that you are allowed to do at one time. Sometimes you may want to do the easier parts first. This way, if you run out of time before you finish, you will have completed a good chunk of the work.

For tests that have a time limit, notice what time it is when the test begins and figure out when you need to stop. Check a few times as you work through the test to be sure you are making good progress and not spending too much time on any particular section.

You don't have to keep up with everyone else. You may notice other students in the class finishing before you do. Don't worry about this. Everyone works at a different pace. Just keep going, trying not to spend too long on any one question.

Fill in answer sheets properly. Even if you know every answer on a test, you won't do well unless you enter the answers correctly on the answer sheet.

Fill in the entire bubble, but don't spend too much time making it perfect. Make your mark dark, but not so dark that it goes through the paper! And be sure you choose only one answer for each question, even if you are not sure. If you choose two answers, both will be marked as wrong.

It's usually not a good idea to change your answers. Usually your first choice is the right one. Unless you realize that you misread the question, the directions, or some facts in a passage, it's usually safer to stay with your first answer. If you are pretty sure it's wrong, of course, go ahead and change it. Make sure you completely erase the first choice and neatly fill in your new choice.

Use context clues to figure out tough questions. If you come across a word or idea you don't understand, use context clues—the words in the sentences nearby— to help you figure out its meaning.

Sometimes it's good to guess. Should you guess when you don't know an answer on a test? That depends. If your teacher has made the test, usually you will score better if you answer as many questions as possible, even if you don't really know the answers.

On standardized tests, here's what to do to score your best. For each question, most of these tests let you choose from four or five answer choices. If you decide that a couple of answers are clearly wrong but you're still not sure about the answer, go ahead and make your best guess. If you can't narrow down the choices at all, then you may be better off skipping the question. Tests like these take away extra points for wrong answers, so it's better to leave them blank. Be sure you skip over the answer space for these questions on the answer sheet, though, so you don't fill in the wrong spaces.

Sometimes you should skip a question and come back to it later.

On many tests, you will score better if you answer more questions. This means that you should not spend too much time on any single question. Sometimes it gets tricky, though, keeping track of questions you skipped on your answer sheet.

If you want to skip a question because you don't know the answer, put a very light pencil mark next to the question in the test booklet. Try to choose an answer, even if you're not sure of it. Fill in the answer lightly on the answer sheet.

Check your work. On a standardized test, you can't go ahead or skip back to another section of the test. But you may go back and review your answers on the section you just worked on if you have extra time.

First, scan your answer sheet. Make sure that you answered every question you could. Also, if you are using a bubble-type answer sheet, make sure that you filled in only one bubble for each question. Erase any extra marks on the page.

Finally—avoid test anxiety! If you get nervous about tests, don't worry. *Test anxiety* happens to lots of good students. Being a little nervous actually sharpens your mind. But if you get very nervous about tests, take a few minutes to relax the night before or the day of the test. One good way to relax is to get some exercise, even if you just have time to stretch, shake out your fingers, and wiggle your toes. If you can't move around, it helps just to take a few slow, deep breaths and picture yourself doing a great job!

Terms to Know

Here's a list of terms that are good to know when taking standardized tests. Don't be worried if you see something new. You may not have learned it in school yet.

acute angle: an angle of less than 90°

adjective: a word that describes a noun (_yellow duckling_, _new bicycle_)

adverb: a word that describes a verb (_ran fast, laughing heartily_)

analogy: a comparison of the relationship between two or more otherwise unrelated things (_Carrot is to vegetable as banana is to fruit._)

angle: the figure formed by two lines that start at the same point, usually shown in degrees

antonyms: words with opposite meanings (_big_ and _small_, _young_ and _old_)

area: the amount of space inside a flat shape, expressed in square units

article: a word such as _a_, _an_, or _the_ that goes in front of a noun (_the_ chicken, _an_ apple)

cause/effect: the reason that something happens

character: a person in a story, book, movie, play, or TV show

compare/contrast: to tell what is alike and different about two or more things

compass rose: the symbol on a map that shows where North, South, East, and West are

conclusion: a logical decision you can make based on information from a reading selection or science experiment

congruent: equal in size or shape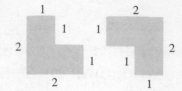

context clues: language and details in a piece of writing that can help you figure out difficult words and ideas

denominator: in a fraction, the number under the line; shows how many equal parts a whole has been divided into ($\frac{1}{2}$, $\frac{6}{7}$)

direct object: in a sentence, the person or thing that receives the action of a verb (_Jane hit the ball hard._)

equation: in math, a statement where one set of numbers or values is equal to another set (_6 + 6 = 12, 4 x 5 = 20_)

factor: a whole number that can be divided exactly into another whole number (_1, 2, 3, 4, and 6 are all factors of 12._)

genre: a category of literature that contains writing with common features (_drama, fiction, nonfiction, poetry_)

hypothesis: in science, the possible answer to a question; most science experiments begin with a hypothesis

indirect object: in a sentence, the noun or pronoun that tells to or for whom the action of the verb is done (_Louise gave a flower to her sister._)

infer: to make an educated guess about a piece of writing, based on information contained in the selection and what you already know

main idea: the most important idea or message in a writing selection

map legend: the part of a map showing symbols that represent natural or human-made objects

noun: a person, place, or thing (*president, underground, train*)

numerator: in a fraction, the number above the line; shows how many equal parts are to be taken from the denominator ($\frac{3}{4}$, $\frac{1}{5}$)

operation: in math, tells what must be done to numbers in an equation (such as add, subtract, multiply, or divide)

parallel: lines or rays that, if extended, could never intersect

percent: fraction of a whole that has been divided into 100 parts, usually expressed with % sign ($\frac{5}{100}$ = 5%)

perimeter: distance around an object or shape

3 ft.

3 ft.   3 ft.

Perimeter =
3 + 3 + 3 + 3 = 12 ft.

3 ft.

perpendicular: lines or rays that intersect to form a 90° (right) angle

90°

predicate: in a sentence, the word or words that tell what the subject does, did, or has (*The fuzzy kitten had black spots on its belly.*)

predict: in science or reading, to use given information to decide what will happen

prefixes/suffixes: letters added to the beginning or end of a word to change its meaning (*reorganize, hopeless*)

preposition: a word that shows the relationship between a noun or pronoun and other words in a phrase or sentence (*We sat by the fire. She walked through the door.*)

probability: the likelihood that something will happen, often shown with numbers

pronoun: a word that is used in place of a noun (*She gave the present to them.*)

ratio: a comparison of two quantities, often shown as a fraction (*The ratio of boys to girls in the class is 2 to 1, or 2/1.*)

sequence: the order in which events happen or in which items can be placed in a pattern

subject: in a sentence, the word or words that tell who or what the sentence is about (*Uncle Robert baked the cake. Everyone at the party ate it.*)

summary: a restatement of important ideas from a selection in the writer's own words

symmetry: in math and science, two or more sides or faces of an object that are mirror images of one another

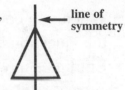

line of symmetry

synonyms: words with the same, or almost the same, meaning (*delicious* and *tasty, funny* and *comical*)

Venn diagram: two or more overlapping circles used to compare and contrast two or more things

square   triangle

• four equal sides
• four 90° angles

• flat shape

• three sides
• three angles

verb: a word that describes an action or state of being (*He watched the fireworks.*)

writing prompt: on a test, a question or statement that you must respond to in writing

Multiple Choice Questions

You have probably seen multiple choice questions before. They are the most common type of question used on standardized tests. To answer a multiple choice question, you must choose one answer from a number of choices.

EXAMPLE	**Cheap has about the same meaning as _____.**
	Ⓐ generous Ⓒ expensive
	Ⓑ stingy Ⓓ charitable

Sometimes you will know the answer right away. But other times you won't. To answer multiple choice questions on a test, do the following:

- First, answer any easy questions whose answers you are *sure* you know.
- When you come to a harder question, circle the question number. You can come back to this question after you have finished all the easier ones.
- Eliminate any answers that you know are wrong. The last choice left is probably the correct one!
- Look for clue words like *same*, *opposite*, *not*, *probably*, *best*, *most likely*, and *main*. They can change the meaning of a question or help you eliminate answer choices.

Testing It Out

Now look at the example question more closely.

Think: I know that I'm looking for a synonym for *cheap*. I think that *cheap* means inexpensive or unwilling to spend money. Choice **A,** *generous*, means giving—that's the opposite of *cheap*.

I'm not sure what *stingy* means, so I'll come back to that one. Choice **C,** *expensive*, means "costs a lot." That's also the opposite of *cheap*, so that can't be the answer.

I'm not sure what *charitable* means, but I think it has something to do with charity, which is giving money away. If you give money away, you're not *cheap*, so that's probably not the answer.

Now back to **B,** *stingy*—this is the only remaining choice. I'll try to use it in a sentence in place of *cheap*. "My brother is really *stingy* when it comes to buying birthday presents." Yes, that makes sense. So I'll choose **B,** *stingy*, as my synonym for *cheap*.

Fill-in-the-Blank Questions

On some tests, you will be given multiple choice questions where you must fill in something that's missing from a phrase, sentence, equation, or passage. These are called fill-in-the-blank questions.

EXAMPLE   **Aaron rides the roller coaster for the feeling of _____ through space.**

    Ⓐ strolling   Ⓒ plummeting

    Ⓑ stirring   Ⓓ plumbing

Directions: To answer fill-in-the-blank questions, do the following:

- Try to think of the answer even before you look at your choices. Even if the answer *is* one of the choices, check the other choices. There may be a better answer.
- Look for the articles *a* and *an* to help you. Since the word *a* must be followed by a consonant and *an* must be followed by words starting with vowel sounds, you can often use articles to eliminate choices.
- For harder questions, try to fit every answer choice into the blank. Which makes sense?
- If you get stuck, try filling in the blank on your own choice (not an answer provided). Then look for synonyms for your new word/words among the answer choices.

Testing It Out

Now look at the example question more closely.

Think: Roller coasters move very quickly; choice **A**, *strolling*, means walking not very fast. So choice **A** doesn't fit.

Choice **B** is *stirring*. I don't think that roller coasters have anything to do with stirring.

Choice **C** is *plummeting*. I think it has something to do with falling. "Aaron rides the roller coaster for the feeling of *falling* through space." That could be right.

Choice **D**, *plumbing*, is a noun that has to do with pipes in your house. That answer choice makes no sense.

So, I think *plummeting* makes the most sense. "Aaron rides the roller coaster for the feeling of *plummeting* through space." I'll choose **C,** *plummeting*, to fill in the blank.

True/False Questions

A true/false question asks you to read a statement and decide if it is right (true) or wrong (false).

EXAMPLE **Every year has 365 days.**

Ⓐ true

Ⓑ false

To answer true/false questions on a test, do the following:

- True/false sections contain more questions than other sections of a test. If there is a time limit on a test, you may need to go more quickly than usual. Do not spend too much time on any one question.
- First, answer all of the easy questions. Circle the numbers next to harder ones and come back to them later.
- If you have time left after completing all the questions, quickly double-check your answers.
- True/false questions with words like *always, never, none, only,* and *every* are usually false. This is because they limit a statement so much.
- True/false questions with words like *most, many,* and *generally* are often true. This is because they make statements more believable.

Testing It Out

Now look at the example question more closely.

Think: I know that 365 is the usual number of days in a year. Why would there be more or fewer days in a year? That's right, there's a leap year every four years. I can't remember how many days there are in a leap year, but it must be different than 365. So I'll answer **F** for false; every year does not have 365 days.

Matching Questions

Matching questions ask you to find words or phrases that are related in a certain way. The choices are often shown in columns.

EXAMPLE   **Match items that mean the same, or almost the same, thing.**

1 indigo	**A** green	1	Ⓐ Ⓑ Ⓒ Ⓓ
2 scarlet	**B** red	2	Ⓐ Ⓑ Ⓒ Ⓓ
3 ebony	**C** black	3	Ⓐ Ⓑ Ⓒ Ⓓ
4 chartreuse	**D** blue	4	Ⓐ Ⓑ Ⓒ Ⓓ

When answering matching questions on tests, follow these guidelines:

- Match the easiest choices first.
- For a difficult word, try using it in a sentence. Then repeat the sentence, substituting your answer choices. The answer that fits best in the sentence is probably the correct one.
- Some matching items contain phrases rather than single words. Begin with the column that has the most words. This column will usually give the most information.
- Work down one column at a time. It is confusing to switch back and forth.

Testing It Out

Now look at the example question more closely.

Think: Both columns contain colors, so I am looking for colors that are the same or closely related. I know that *indigo* comes after blue in the rainbow, so it must be either a kind of blue or purple. Since purple is not a choice, I'll match *indigo* to **D,** *blue.*

I'm pretty sure that *scarlet* is a kind of red, so the answer to number 2 is **B.**

I'm not sure what color *ebony* is, but I think it might be a kind of wood, and I've heard it used to describe keys on a piano. So it could be either black or white, but black makes more sense. I'll choose **C.**

The last item in the column is *chartreuse*, but I have no idea what that means. However, green is the only remaining choice and I'm fairly certain of my other answers. So I'll match 4, *chartreuse*, to **A,** *green.*

Analogy Questions

Analogies ask you to figure out the relationship between two things. Then you must complete another pair with the same relationship.

EXAMPLE	**Contented is to uneasy as thoughtless is to _____.**
	Ⓐ generous Ⓒ rude
	Ⓑ considerate Ⓓ mournful

Analogies usually have two pairs of items. In the question above, the two pairs are *contented/uneasy* and *thoughtless/ _____ .* To answer analogy questions on standardized tests, do the following:

• First, figure out how the first pair of items relate to each other. Try to form a sentence that explains how they are related.

• Next, use your sentence to figure out the missing word in the second pair of items.

• For more difficult analogies, try each answer choice in the sentence you formed.

• Decide if you are looking for a noun, verb, adjective, or other part of speech. If the first pair of words are nouns and the word you are looking to match is a noun, you're probably looking for a noun. So you can eliminate any choices that are not nouns.

Testing It Out
Now look at the example question more closely.

Think: How are *contented* and *uneasy* related? "*Contented* and *uneasy* are antonyms." So I am looking for the opposite of *thoughtless*.

A, *generous*, means giving. I guess this is very different from being *thoughtless*; perhaps it is even an antonym. This may be the answer.

I think that **B,** *mournful*, means sad. It's not really an antonym.

C, *rude*, is similar in meaning to *thoughtless*. It is not an antonym.

I know that **D,** *considerate*, means to be thoughtful. So *considerate* is definitely an antonym for *thoughtless*. So I'll choose **D,** *considerate*, as my answer.

Answer Sheet

Name _____

Practice Test Answer Sheet

Fill in **only one** letter for each item. If you change an answer, make sure to erase your first mark completely.

Unit 1: Reading, pages 15-29

A Ⓐ Ⓑ Ⓒ Ⓓ	7 Ⓐ Ⓑ Ⓒ Ⓓ	15 Ⓐ Ⓑ Ⓒ Ⓓ	C Ⓐ Ⓑ Ⓒ Ⓓ	29 Ⓕ Ⓖ Ⓗ Ⓙ
B Ⓕ Ⓖ Ⓗ Ⓙ	8 Ⓕ Ⓖ Ⓗ Ⓙ	16 Ⓕ Ⓖ Ⓗ Ⓙ	23 Ⓐ Ⓑ Ⓒ Ⓓ	30 Ⓐ Ⓑ Ⓒ Ⓓ
1 Ⓐ Ⓑ Ⓒ Ⓓ	9 Ⓐ Ⓑ Ⓒ Ⓓ	17 Ⓐ Ⓑ Ⓒ Ⓓ	24 Ⓕ Ⓖ Ⓗ Ⓙ	31 Ⓕ Ⓖ Ⓗ Ⓙ
2 Ⓕ Ⓖ Ⓗ Ⓙ	10 Ⓕ Ⓖ Ⓗ Ⓙ	18 Ⓕ Ⓖ Ⓗ Ⓙ	25 Ⓐ Ⓑ Ⓒ Ⓓ	32 Ⓐ Ⓑ Ⓒ Ⓓ
3 Ⓐ Ⓑ Ⓒ Ⓓ	11 Ⓐ Ⓑ Ⓒ Ⓓ	19 Ⓐ Ⓑ Ⓒ Ⓓ	26 Ⓕ Ⓖ Ⓗ Ⓙ	33 Ⓕ Ⓖ Ⓗ Ⓙ
4 Ⓕ Ⓖ Ⓗ Ⓙ	12 Ⓕ Ⓖ Ⓗ Ⓙ	20 Ⓕ Ⓖ Ⓗ Ⓙ	27 Ⓐ Ⓑ Ⓒ Ⓓ	
5 Ⓐ Ⓑ Ⓒ Ⓓ	13 Ⓐ Ⓑ Ⓒ Ⓓ	21 Ⓐ Ⓑ Ⓒ Ⓓ	D Ⓐ Ⓑ Ⓒ Ⓓ	
6 Ⓕ Ⓖ Ⓗ Ⓙ	14 Ⓕ Ⓖ Ⓗ Ⓙ	22 Ⓕ Ⓖ Ⓗ Ⓙ	28 Ⓐ Ⓑ Ⓒ Ⓓ	

Unit 2: Language Arts, pages 30-40

A Ⓐ Ⓑ Ⓒ Ⓓ	11 Ⓐ Ⓑ Ⓒ Ⓓ	E Ⓕ Ⓖ Ⓗ Ⓙ	34 Ⓕ Ⓖ Ⓗ Ⓙ
1 Ⓐ Ⓑ Ⓒ Ⓓ	12 Ⓕ Ⓖ Ⓗ Ⓙ	23 Ⓕ Ⓖ Ⓗ Ⓙ Ⓚ	35 Ⓐ Ⓑ Ⓒ Ⓓ
2 Ⓕ Ⓖ Ⓗ Ⓙ	13 Ⓐ Ⓑ Ⓒ Ⓓ	24 Ⓐ Ⓑ Ⓒ Ⓓ Ⓔ	36 Ⓕ Ⓖ Ⓗ Ⓙ Ⓚ
B Ⓐ Ⓑ Ⓒ Ⓓ	14 Ⓕ Ⓖ Ⓗ Ⓙ	F Ⓐ Ⓑ Ⓒ Ⓓ	37 Ⓐ Ⓑ Ⓒ Ⓓ
3 Ⓐ Ⓑ Ⓒ Ⓓ	15 Ⓐ Ⓑ Ⓒ Ⓓ	25 Ⓐ Ⓑ Ⓒ Ⓓ	38 Ⓕ Ⓖ Ⓗ Ⓙ
4 Ⓕ Ⓖ Ⓗ Ⓙ	16 Ⓕ Ⓖ Ⓗ Ⓙ	26 Ⓕ Ⓖ Ⓗ Ⓙ	39 Ⓐ Ⓑ Ⓒ Ⓓ
5 Ⓐ Ⓑ Ⓒ Ⓓ	17 Ⓐ Ⓑ Ⓒ Ⓓ	27 Ⓐ Ⓑ Ⓒ Ⓓ	40 Ⓕ Ⓖ Ⓗ Ⓙ
6 Ⓕ Ⓖ Ⓗ Ⓙ	18 Ⓕ Ⓖ Ⓗ Ⓙ	28 Ⓕ Ⓖ Ⓗ Ⓙ	41 Ⓐ Ⓑ Ⓒ Ⓓ Ⓔ
7 Ⓐ Ⓑ Ⓒ Ⓓ	19 Ⓐ Ⓑ Ⓒ Ⓓ	29 Ⓐ Ⓑ Ⓒ Ⓓ	42 Ⓕ Ⓖ Ⓗ Ⓙ Ⓚ
8 Ⓕ Ⓖ Ⓗ Ⓙ	D Ⓐ Ⓑ Ⓒ Ⓓ	30 Ⓕ Ⓖ Ⓗ Ⓙ	43 Ⓐ Ⓑ Ⓒ Ⓓ Ⓔ
9 Ⓐ Ⓑ Ⓒ Ⓓ	20 Ⓐ Ⓑ Ⓒ Ⓓ	31 Ⓐ Ⓑ Ⓒ Ⓓ	44 Ⓕ Ⓖ Ⓗ Ⓙ Ⓚ
10 Ⓕ Ⓖ Ⓗ Ⓙ	21 Ⓕ Ⓖ Ⓗ Ⓙ	32 Ⓕ Ⓖ Ⓗ Ⓙ	
C Ⓐ Ⓑ Ⓒ Ⓓ	22 Ⓐ Ⓑ Ⓒ Ⓓ	33 Ⓐ Ⓑ Ⓒ Ⓓ	

Name _____

Practice Test Answer Sheet

Unit 3: Mathematics, pages 41-50

A Ⓐ Ⓑ Ⓒ Ⓓ Ⓔ   7 Ⓐ Ⓑ Ⓒ Ⓓ   16 Ⓕ Ⓖ Ⓗ Ⓙ Ⓚ   24 Ⓐ Ⓑ Ⓒ Ⓓ

B Ⓕ Ⓖ Ⓗ Ⓙ Ⓚ   8 Ⓕ Ⓖ Ⓗ Ⓙ   17 Ⓐ Ⓑ Ⓒ Ⓓ Ⓔ   25 Ⓕ Ⓖ Ⓗ Ⓙ

1 Ⓐ Ⓑ Ⓒ Ⓓ Ⓔ   9 Ⓐ Ⓑ Ⓒ Ⓓ   18 Ⓕ Ⓖ Ⓗ Ⓙ Ⓚ   26 Ⓐ Ⓑ Ⓒ Ⓓ

2 Ⓕ Ⓖ Ⓗ Ⓙ Ⓚ   10 Ⓕ Ⓖ Ⓗ Ⓙ   19 Ⓐ Ⓑ Ⓒ Ⓓ Ⓔ   27 Ⓕ Ⓖ Ⓗ Ⓙ

3 Ⓐ Ⓑ Ⓒ Ⓓ Ⓔ   11 Ⓐ Ⓑ Ⓒ Ⓓ   20 Ⓕ Ⓖ Ⓗ Ⓙ Ⓚ   28 Ⓐ Ⓑ Ⓒ Ⓓ

4 Ⓕ Ⓖ Ⓗ Ⓙ Ⓚ   12 Ⓕ Ⓖ Ⓗ Ⓙ   21 Ⓐ Ⓑ Ⓒ Ⓓ Ⓔ   29 Ⓕ Ⓖ Ⓗ Ⓙ

C Ⓐ Ⓑ Ⓒ Ⓓ   13 Ⓐ Ⓑ Ⓒ Ⓓ   D Ⓐ Ⓑ Ⓒ Ⓓ   30 Ⓐ Ⓑ Ⓒ Ⓓ

5 Ⓐ Ⓑ Ⓒ Ⓓ   14 Ⓕ Ⓖ Ⓗ Ⓙ   22 Ⓐ Ⓑ Ⓒ Ⓓ   31 Ⓕ Ⓖ Ⓗ Ⓙ

6 Ⓕ Ⓖ Ⓗ Ⓙ   15 Ⓐ Ⓑ Ⓒ Ⓓ   23 Ⓕ Ⓖ Ⓗ Ⓙ

Name _____

Reading

Lesson 1 Reading Nonfiction

SAMPLE A

Walking briskly has been called the perfect exercise. If you keep up the pace and move your arms actively, you burn up calories and tone your muscles. In one respect, walking is even better than running—you aren't as likely to hurt your feet, knees, or lower back.

In this passage, the writer talks about "walking briskly." The word *briskly* probably means

A by yourself.

B with others.

C quickly.

D slowly.

SAMPLE B

Which sentence would best follow the last sentence in the passage?

F Best of all, walking is free.

G Another good sport is swimming.

H Back problems affect many people.

J Even so, people still run.

TIPS

Skim the story, then skim the questions. Answer the easiest questions first. Most answers can be checked in the story.

Look for key words in the question or the answer you think is right. Find these words in the story and you'll be able to check your answer.

Getting Around

In today's world, there are countless ways to travel, from space shuttles to plain old walking. In this part of the book, you'll read about two very different ways of getting around, one new and one very old.

GO

Name _____

Directions: Patricia wrote this report for a school project. She knew the topic well because she had just been on a school trip to England. Read the report, then do numbers 1–11.

Destination Europe

Airline travel is becoming so affordable and easy that many people are deciding to take vacations to far-away places, especially Europe. Flying to a foreign country is very different from flying from one American city to another, however, so it is important to prepare carefully.

Before taking an international flight, travelers must decide where they are going and when they want to go. Different countries are more enjoyable at certain times of the year. Then travelers must make a reservation and buy their tickets from a travel agent or airline. During busy times of the year, these steps must be taken several weeks or even months before the trip.

All international travelers need a passport, a legal document that lets them enter foreign countries and return to America. Passports look like thin, small books, with the traveler's home country written on the front. Inside is a picture of the person and important information about the traveler. In many respects, a passport is like a hall pass. Instead of letting you walk around school, it lets you travel in foreign countries.

Most airlines let each person bring only two suitcases, so travelers should choose carefully what to take with them. Of course, clothes and personal items are necessary. Since other countries use different kinds of money, most travelers buy some of the foreign money before leaving home. Flights from the United States to Europe last about nine hours, so it's a good idea to bring a book or a game to play to pass the time. Some planes fly overnight, so passengers can sleep part of the time.

On the day of the trip, travelers should arrive at the airport with their suitcases and tickets, along with their passports. The airline agent will exchange the ticket for a boarding pass and send the suitcases to a handler, who will put them on the plane. The agent will also check each passport to be sure everything is in order. Travelers then go to their gates and wait for the flights. Recently, some airlines have stopped giving paper tickets and started doing their ticketing electronically. This saves paper and time, and passengers like it because they can't lose their tickets.

Name _____

As people board the plane, they find the seats on their boarding passes and put their carry-on bags in a safe place. No plane can take off until the passengers are in their seats with their seat belts fastened. Airplane seats have high backs and armrests, like big armchairs. Some airline seats have plugs for headphones so passengers can listen to music. These headphones may also be used to enjoy a movie shown on a big screen. The newest planes even have a small video screen for each passenger.

The inside of an airplane looks a little like a big, fancy bus. The pilot and crew are in a little room at the front. The passengers sit in rows with a wide walkway down the middle. A small part of the plane is for the flight attendants, and there are also bathrooms.

Large planes have several flight attendants, who are there to make the flight safe and comfortable. When it is time to eat, flight attendants bring meals, which are served on small fold-down trays. These trays can also be used for other things, like playing cards. Some airline seats are next to the windows, giving passengers who sit in them a real bird's-eye view of the ground.

The most difficult thing about traveling to Europe is the time change. As the plane flies, it crosses time zones. Imagine that you leave New York at lunchtime and arrive in Paris, France, eight hours later. Your watch tells you it's time for dinner, but in Paris, it's 4:00 in the morning and most people in France are asleep. To remind you to change your watch, the pilot announces the local time before the flight ends.

Once the plane has landed, the suitcases are taken to an area of the airport called Customs. This is where special airport workers look at what travelers bring into the country. Then, after a passport check, the travelers are free to begin their visit.

As you can see, international air travel can be fun and exciting, as long as travelers plan ahead and know what to expect.

1 **Which picture shows what a passport looks like?**

A

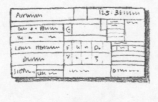
B

C

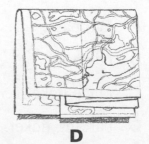
D

GO

Name _____

2 Travelers need a passport to

   F enter their own country after a trip.

   G leave their seats in the airplane.

   H get their baggage after arriving.

   J choose the dates they plan to travel.

3 This passage is mostly about

   A what happens in an airport.

   B taking a flight to another country.

   C flying in the United States.

   D the cost of international travel.

4 From what you read, which of the following looks most like an airplane seat?

    F   **G**   **H**   **J**

5 The author compares a passport to a

   A hall pass.

   B bus pass.

   C plane ticket.

   D parking ticket.

GO

Name _____

6 The author of the passage would probably agree that international airline travel

F is too complicated.

G costs too much money.

H is usually frightening.

J can be fun and exciting.

7 Which of these statements about the passage best supports your answer choice for number 6?

A The passage is mostly about travel to distant places.

B The passage is mostly about living in a distant place.

C The passage is mostly about different ways to travel.

D The passage is mostly about airport terminals.

8 The author says that "no plane can take off until the passengers are in their seats with their seat belts fastened." The words *take off* probably mean

F come back.

G start the engine.

H stop moving.

J leave the ground.

9 Which idea helps you know that your answer to number 8 is right?

A Before the plane goes up in the air, passengers must be wearing their seat belts.

B Some planes have video screens for each passenger.

C Airline seats are a little like armchairs.

D Each airline seat has a seat belt, and some have headphones.

10 The author says that "As people board the plane, they find the seats on their boarding passes and put their carry-on bags in a safe place." The word *board* probably means

F walk around.

G get into.

H get out of.

J stand on.

11 If you wanted to learn more about the topic of the passage, which of these books would be most useful?

A *Train Guide to Europe*

B *International Travel Guide*

C *Flying Cheaply in the U.S.A.*

D *How to Get a Job With an Airline*

GO

Name _____

Directions: Some of Patricia's friends wrote about travel experiences they had. These questions are about their writing.

12 **In which of these resources could Marty find information about travel agents in his town?**

   F   **G**   **H**   **J**

13 **Julia is reading an article about planes. Under which of these headings in the article should she look to find out what kinds of fuel different planes use?**

  A Types of Engines

  B Types of Wings

  C Landing a Plane

  D Steering a Plane

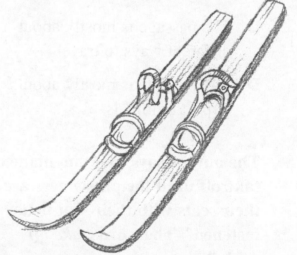

14 **Which of the sentences below best combines these two sentences into one?**

My brother has antique skis.
The antique skis are made of wood.

  F Made of wood, my brother has antique skis.

  G My brother has antique skis and the skis are made of wood.

  H My brother has antique skis made of wood.

  J Antique skis made of wood my brother has.

GO

Test Prep

Name _____

Directions: More than 70 years ago, an American athlete did something most everyone thought was impossible. This is the story of that great athlete and her accomplishment. Read the story, then do numbers 15–22.

First Lady of Swimming

Thousands of people cross the channel of water between France and England every day in planes, ferries, and even trains. An American athlete, Gertrude Caroline Ederle, however, used a different method. She was the first woman to swim across the English Channel.

Gertrude Ederle was born in New York City in 1906. She dedicated herself to the sport of swimming at an early age and enjoyed great success. Before long, she was on her way to becoming one of the most famous American swimmers of her time. When she was sixteen, Ederle broke seven records in one day at a swimming competition in New York. Two years later, in 1924, she represented the United States at the Olympic Games, winning a gold medal in the 400-meter freestyle relay.

After her Olympic victory, she looked for an even greater challenge. One of the most difficult swims is to cross the 21-mile English Channel. The seas in the channel can be rough, and the water is cold. In the past, the feat had only been accomplished by male swimmers. Most people believed that the swim was too difficult for a woman, but Ederle wanted to prove them wrong. She didn't make it on her first attempt, but in 1926 she tried again. Leaving from the coast of France, Ederle had to swim even longer than planned because of heavy seas. She went an extra fourteen miles and still managed to beat the world record by almost two hours. This accomplishment made her an instant heroine at the age of twenty.

After her triumph, Ederle traveled around the United States as a professional swimmer, delighting spectators of all ages. Unfortunately, a severe back injury kept her out of the pool for four years. It wasn't until 1939 that she swam in public again, in a swimming show at the New York World's Fair.

Later in life, Ederle worked as a swimming instructor for hearing-impaired children. She was also appointed to President Eisenhower's Youth Fitness Committee. Her dedication to the sport of swimming has made Gertrude Ederle a role model for athletes ever since. Because of her willingness to accept enormous challenges, she is a good example for anyone who wants to excel.

GO

15 According to the passage, why did Ederle decide to swim across the English Channel?

A There weren't ferries across the Channel then.

B She wanted to be the first woman to do it.

C She wanted the attention it would bring her.

D A friend had dared her to do it.

16 Which of these best describes why Ederle swam farther than 21 miles to cross the English Channel?

F There were heavy seas that day.

G She wanted to show off for the spectators.

H Her start was slow, then she lost confidence.

J She got lost because of the fog.

17 How did the public react after Ederle broke the world record for the swim across the English Channel?

A They all wanted to do it, too.

B They admired her courage and dedication.

C They thought she hadn't really done it.

D They wanted her to do it again.

18 Which of these is not one of Gertrude Ederle's accomplishments?

F winning a gold medal in the Olympic Games

G swimming in the coldest water in the world

H breaking a world record for swimming the English Channel

J being appointed to a presidential committee

GO

Name _____

19 Which definition of the word *beat* is used in this sentence from the passage?

> She went an extra fourteen miles and still managed to beat the world record by almost two hours.

A to whip, like eggs

B to be faster than

C to hit, like a carpet

D the tempo of music

20 What does the author mean by the sentence reprinted in number 19?

F Setting world records isn't as important as swimming far.

G Miss Ederle failed to set a new record because she went too far.

H She was two hours late, and therefore didn't set the record.

J Miss Ederle set a new record even though she swam too far.

21 What is the main idea of the passage?

A Swimming can be a very profitable sport.

B Hard work and dedication can lead to great success.

C It's never too late to start learning something new.

D People who compete in the Olympics usually go far.

22 Here is a paragraph about another swimmer. Which sentence does not belong in the paragraph?

F Sentence 1

G Sentence 2

H Sentence 3

J Sentence 4

[1]Sara Fernandez is a young athlete who has been swimming since she was six. [2]She also learned to ride a bike when she was young. [3]Sara has to use a wheelchair, but she has become a great swimmer. [4]Recently, she went to the state swimming championships and won two silver medals.

STOP

Name _____

Lesson 2 Reading Fiction

SAMPLE C

The ski instructor helped Danny stand up. He gave Danny a little push, and the boy began sliding down the mountain. Just when Danny thought he would fall, the instructor caught him.

This is probably Danny's

A only vacation.

B last day of school.

C first time skiing.

D first time in the snow.

TIPS

If a question seems difficult, look at the answer choices, then read the question again.

As soon as you know which answer is right, mark it and go on to the next item. Check your answers only after you have tried all the items.

Directions: Here is a story about a family that is taking an exciting vacation, one that you might enjoy. Read the story and then do numbers 23–27.

Floating the River

"Aren't we there yet?" Shiloh asked. At last, she and her family were on their way to their annual tubing trip. Floating down Glenn River on an inner tube was one of Shiloh's favorite things. She was sure this year's trip would be the best ever. They would float five whole miles, all the way to Glenn Fork. They planned to stop along the way to eat their lunches, but only if the lunches stayed dry in their waterproof packs! There would also be time for swimming, another thing Shiloh loved to do.

With each passing mile, Shiloh smiled more and more as she thought of the fun they would have. When they finally reached Glenn Fork and parked the car, she jumped out, all ready to go.

GO

"Not so fast, Shiloh," said her mother. "Remember, we're just here to leave the car. We still have to drive up the river. After we float back here, we'll be able to drive the car upstream to the truck. Otherwise, we won't have any way to get home."

"Oh, yeah, false alarm," Shiloh said. She had forgotten the family's plan to leave one car at each end of the float.

Once the whole family was in the truck, they set out for Jenkins Bar, a sandy beach on a wide part of the river. It didn't take very long to get there on the road. But because of the river's many winding turns and slow current, it would take them about three hours to float back to Glenn Fork. "That's three wonderful hours of tubing," thought Shiloh, "and the fun is about to begin."

Shiloh's father helped her unload her backpack and shiny tube from the truck. Once everyone was ready, they left the truck and walked down to the river's bank. They all put their toes in the water, and Shiloh gasped as she felt how cold the water was. Since she was a little taller and stronger this time, she wasn't as afraid of the river's current. She remembered having to hold her mother's hand last year, the way her little sister was doing now. Shiloh took a deep breath and pushed herself out into the river. As she followed her family downstream, she thought to herself, "This will be the best tubing trip ever!"

23 **In the story, Shiloh decides that getting out of the car at Glenn Fork was a "false alarm." In this case, a *false alarm* is a**

A warning

C misunderstanding

B funny story

D mistake

GO

Name _____

24 **Why does Shiloh think that this year's trip will be the best ever?**

    F Her family has started down the river without her.

    G She is stronger and less afraid now.

    H They have decided to leave a car at each end of the trip.

    J She gets to carry her own tube and backpack.

25 **By the end of the passage, Shiloh's feelings have changed from**

    A (sadness) → (happiness)

    B (boredom) → (sadness)

    C (fear) → (impatience)

    D (impatience) → (excitement)

26 **This story is mostly about**

    F driving a car and a truck.

    G a one-day adventure.

    H a tiresome journey.

    J being older and stronger.

27 **The members of Shiloh's family seem to**

    A get along well.

    B worry about the weather.

    C compete with each other.

    D have long discussions.

STOP

Name _____

Lesson 3   Review

[1] My grandfather us visits almost every week. [2] He lives in a small town about an hour away.

Choose the best way to rewrite Sentence 1.

A Every week, my grandfather almost visits us.

C My grandfather, who visits us almost every week.

B My grandfather visits us almost every week.

D Almost every week, my grandfather visiting us.

Directions: Here is a daily journal written by a young boy visiting his cousins. There are several mistakes that need correcting.

Monday, April 16

[1] Today I arrived in Glen Mill to stay with my cousins. [2] They live in a big house on a farm. [3] There are a lot of animals to care for and other things to do. [4] Farms usually have a main house, a barn, and lots of land. [5] Tomorrow I'll get to help with the calves. [6] We'll also make homemade jam. [7] It sounds like life on a farm is more busier than life in the city.

28 **Which is the best way to write Sentence 3?**

A There being a lot of animals to take care of and things to do.

B There is a lot of animals to take care of and things to do.

C Being a lot of animals to take care of and things to do.

D Best as it is

29 **Which sentence does not belong in the paragraph?**

F Sentence 1

G Sentence 4

H Sentence 5

J Sentence 7

GO

Name _____

Journal

Wednesday, April 18

[1]Today was very busy. [2]Jane, Carl, and I went out around 8:00 to fill our buckets with blackberries. [3]It was hard work, and we didn't get back until it was time for lunch. [4]This afternoon, Aunt Mara showed us how to wash and sort the berries. [5]She did the cooking part, but she let us fill the jars and decorate the labels. [6]Now Aunt Mara is letting me take a jar of jam home for Mom she'll be surprised I made it. [7]I hope the rest of my stay here is as much fun as today was.

30 **Which sentence contains two complete thoughts and should be written as two sentences?**

A Sentence 1

B Sentence 3

C Sentence 5

D Sentence 6

31 **If students wanted to find out more information about life on a farm, it would be most helpful to look**

F in an encyclopedia under "calves."

G in a dictionary under "farming."

H in an atlas under the heading "Glen Mill."

J in a book about farm life.

GO

Name _____

Directions: On this page, you will read about a girl named Rachel who lives on a very different kind of farm. Here are two paragraphs about where she lives.

32   **Choose the sentence that best fills the blank in the paragraph.**

> People laugh when I tell them what kind of farm we have. My family raises catfish! _____. We feed them pellets that look almost like the food you feed cats or dogs.

A   Then the fish are sent to a store.

B   The fish live in ponds on our farm.

C   Before we raised cows and sheep.

D   Even my little brother helps out.

33   **Rachel wrote about how her family's catfish farm works. Choose the sentence that best fills the blank in the paragraph.**

> A big tank truck filled with water comes to the farm. Inside the truck are thousands of baby catfish. The truck backs up to the edge of a pond. _____. My mother and I hold the other end in the pond. The truck driver opens up the tank, and the fish go from the tank into the pond.

F   Then my father hooks one end of a big hose up to the truck.

G   However, the driver is very busy.

H   Each of us does a different thing.

J   Afterward, the driver moves the truck to another pond.

STOP

Name _____

Language Arts

Lesson 1 Vocabulary

Directions: For Sample A and numbers 1 and 2, read the sentences. Choose the word that correctly completes both sentences.

Directions: For Sample B and numbers 3 and 4, choose the word that means the **opposite** of the underlined word.

SAMPLE A

Is this your _____ of gum?
Gerry will _____ her bags.

A stick

B pack

C move

D piece

SAMPLE B

<u>bitter</u> taste

A strange

B sweet

C dull

D pleasant

1 I threw the _____ at the target.
The bird _____ from the tree.

A darts   **C** flies

B balls   **D** jumps

2 Will you _____ the cheese for me?
A _____ covered the opening.

F slice   **H** buy

G lid   **J** grate

3 <u>harvest</u> vegetables

A eat   **C** pick

B cook   **D** plant

4 sleepy <u>driver</u>

F cyclist   **H** passenger

G child   **J** officer

Use the meaning of a sentence to find the answer.

Think about the meaning of the answer choices.

GO

Name _____

Directions: For numbers 5 and 6, read the sentences with the missing word and the question about that word. Choose the word that best answers the question.

5 This is the _____ part of the project. Which word means it was the first part of the project?

   A final   **C** reasonable

   B initial   **D** challenging

6 Louis had to _____ the floor. Which word means Louis had to clean the floor very well?

   F scrub   **H** deposit

   G rinse   **J** replace

Directions: For numbers 7 and 8, choose the word that means the same, or about the same, as the underlined word.

7 tiny <u>particle</u>

   A animal

   B package

   C piece

   D gift

8 <u>assist</u> him

   F bother

   G help

   H hinder

   J join

Directions: For numbers 9 and 10, read the paragraph. For each numbered blank, there is a list of words with the same number. Choose the word from each list that best completes the meaning of the paragraph.

One of the most ____(9)____ books ever written almost went unpublished. Margaret Mitchell's novel *Gone with the Wind* was rejected by several editors. Eventually, it was published and received a Pulitzer Prize. Mitchell's epic about the Civil War became the best-selling book in American publishing history and was later turned into an ____(10)____ successful movie.

9 **A** humorous   **C** recent   **10** **F** internally   **H** emotionally

     B famous   **D** difficult   **G** equally   **J** originally

STOP

Name _____

Lesson 2 Language Mechanics

Directions: For Sample C and numbers 11–14, look at the underlined part of the sentence. Choose the answer that shows the best capitalization and punctuation for that part.

SAMPLE C The library will be closed this <u>week. It</u> will open again on Monday.

    A week. it

    B Week, it

    C week it

    D Correct as it is

---

11 <u>Mom: don't you</u> want me to go with you to the store?

    A Mom. Don't you

    B Mom? don't you

    C Mom, don't you

    D Correct as it is

12 While you were gone, Mr. Taylor <u>said "the party</u> starts at noon."

    F said The party

    G said, "The party

    H said, "the party

    J Correct as it is

13 Marisa has to go to the dentist <u>today But</u> she would rather stay home.

    A today, but

    B today. but

    C today; but

    D Correct as it is

14 On our trip to the beach, we found <u>rocks, shells, and starfish.</u>

    F rocks shells and starfish.

    G rocks, shells, and, starfish.

    H rocks, shells and, starfish.

    J Correct as it is

Compare the answer choices carefully.

Ask yourself: "Am I looking for a mistake or correct capitalization and punctuation?"

GO

Name _____

Directions: For numbers 15 and 16, choose the answer that is written correctly and shows the correct capitalization and punctuation.

15
A How can Anthony stand to sleep for so long.

B Babies spend a lot of time sleeping

C When the alarm rings, try to wake up?

D We like to sleep outside in the summer.

16
F Which boy didnt enter the photo contest?

G Angela can't see the winning photos from here.

H Mrs. Johnsons' class won first place in the contest.

J My cousin's always take photos on their vacation.

Directions: For numbers 17–19, read the letter and the underlined parts. Choose the answer that shows the best capitalization and punctuation for each part.

(17) November, 5 2001

(18) Dear Juan

    I am sorry I missed your party last week. I had already been invited to my aunt's house by the Nueces River, we had a good time. Thanks for the invitation anyway.

(19) Your friend;

Nancy

17
A november 5, 2001

B November 5, 2001

C November 5 2001

D Correct as it is

18
F Dear Juan,

G dear Juan,

H Dear Juan:

J Correct as it is

19
A Your friend,

B Your Friend

C your friend

D Correct as it is

STOP

Name _____

Lesson 3   Spelling

Directions: For Sample D and numbers 20–22, choose the word that is spelled correctly and best completes the sentence.

Directions: For Sample E and numbers 23 and 24, read each phrase. Find the underlined word that is not spelled correctly. If all the underlined words are spelled correctly, mark "All correct."

SAMPLE D   The sports _____ is next week.

   A banquet

   B banqet

   C banguet

   D bancquet

SAMPLE E

   A not <u>allowed</u>

   B <u>youngest</u> child

   C funny <u>clown</u>

   D small <u>scratch</u>

   E All correct

20 Jenny _____ the math test.

   A paist   **C** passed

   B passded   **D** passted

21 Peter _____ his shirt before going to the party.

   F ironed   **H** iorned

   G ierned   **J** irnded

22 The hikers _____ the poison ivy.

   A uvoided   **C** avoided

   B evoided   **D** avoidid

23 **F** hotel <u>lobby</u>

   G famous <u>auther</u>

   H <u>steering</u> wheel

   J strange <u>journey</u>

   K All correct

24 **A** <u>wrinkled</u> shirt

   B <u>nursery</u> school

   C young <u>coach</u>

   D <u>useless</u> idea

   E All correct

Don't spend too much time looking at the words. Pretty soon, they all begin to look like they are spelled wrong.

STOP

Lesson 4   Writing

Directions: Read the paragraph about one student's mixed feelings about going
to a new school.

I have mixed feelings about going to a new school. I miss my friends from my old
school, and I miss the city where we lived before. Still, this school is newer, and it even
has a new gym. I'm making new friends here, and I can take classes I couldn't take at my
old school.

Directions: Now think about something you have mixed feelings about. Write one or two
sentences to answer each question below, and then use your answers to write a paragraph
of your own.

What do you have mixed feelings about?

_____

What do you dislike about it? Why?

_____

_____

_____

What do you like about it? Why?

_____

_____

_____

Write your own paragraph on the lines below.

_____

_____

_____

_____

GO

Name _____

Directions: Read the short story about one child's problem.

Misha stood on the stage. His knees knocked. His heart pounded. His palms were drenched. His hands shook so hard that he could barely hold his violin. A hush fell over the audience. Hundreds of eyes bored holes through Misha. He couldn't move to leave, but he didn't want to stay.

In the wings, he heard his friend whisper. "You can do it. Take a deep breath. Close your eyes. Pretend that you're standing in your den."

Misha shut his eyes tight. In his mind, he saw the pictures on the wall in his den. He lifted the violin to his chin and played his solo perfectly from beginning to end.

Directions: Now think about a fiction story that you would like to write. Write one or two sentences to answer each question below, and then use your answers to write a paragraph of your own.

Think about your main character. Who is it? What is he or she like?

_____

_____

What is the setting of the story?

_____

_____

What kind of problem will the main character have? How will the character solve the problem?

_____

_____

Write your own short story on the lines below.

_____

_____

_____

STOP

Name _____

Lesson 5 Review

Directions: For Sample F and number 25, read the sentences. Choose the word that correctly completes **both** sentences.

SAMPLE F

The dog caught the _____.
Our school has a formal _____.

> **A** ball   **B** dance   **C** stick   **D** event

25 The _____ climbed the tree.
I can't _____ this heat.

A fox   **C** cat

B stand   **D** bear

Directions: For numbers 26 and 27, read the sentences with the missing word. Choose the word that best answers the question.

26 We hiked to a _____ campsite. Which word means the campsite was far away?

F remote   **H** crowded

G pleasant   **J** level

27 Joe's _____ will be remembered. Which word means what Joe said will be remembered?

A adjustment   **C** resource

B remark   **D** impatience

Directions: For number 28, choose the word that means the **opposite** of the underlined word.

28 <u>collect</u> money

F discover   **H** distribute

G spend   **J** save

Directions: For numbers 29 and 30, choose the word that means the same, or about the same, as the underlined word.

29 <u>depart</u> soon

A leave   **C** study

B win   **D** detect

30 <u>miniature</u> house

F huge   **H** expensive

G tiny   **J** unusual

GO

Directions: For numbers 31 and 32, choose the answer that is written correctly and shows the correct capitalization and punctuation.

31 **A** Chip shouted "I found the book here under my bed!"

  B "Are books always so long" he asked.

  C Madeleine said, "Please bring me my book, Daddy."

  D Our teacher always says, "don't leave your books at home.

32 **F** "Roller coasters scare me, but they're fun, he whispered.

  G Nouria shouted "it's the biggest roller coaster in the country!"

  H My mom said, you're too young to go on the roller coaster.

  J "Let's go on the roller coaster," Jeremy suggested.

Directions: For numbers 33–36, read the paragraph and the underlined parts. Choose the answer that shows the best capitalization and punctuation for each part.

(33) We are reading an article called <u>Food For Thought</u>.
(34) It is about what we should and <u>shouldnt</u> eat as snacks.
(35) Some of the ideas in the article are very <u>good like</u> choosing an apple instead of chips. The article
(36) made me <u>think; but</u> it also made me hungry.

33 **A** "Food for Thought."

  B "food for thought."

  C food for thought.

  D Correct as it is

35 **A** good. Like

  B good Like

  C good, like

  D Correct as it is

34 **F** shouldn't

  G should'nt

  H shouldnt'

  J Correct as it is

36 **F** think, But

  G think, but

  H think but

  J Correct as it is

GO

Directions: For numbers 37–40, choose the word that is spelled correctly and best completes the sentence.

37 **We'll be _____ after this run.**

   A thirsdy

   B thirsty

   C thursty

   D thirstie

38 **We were in a harmless _____ yesterday.**

   F accident

   G acident

   H accidint

   J accadent

39 **Make sure to _____ the cans from the bottles.**

   A seperate   **C** separat

   B sepparate   **D** separate

40 **Please _____ me when you get home.**

   F tellephone   **H** telefone

   G telaphone   **J** telephone

Directions: For numbers 41–44, read each phrase. Find the underlined word that is **not** spelled correctly. If all the underlined words are spelled correctly, mark "All correct."

41 **A** <u>crowded</u> stadium

   B <u>memorize</u> words

   C <u>substitute</u> teacher

   D <u>ancient</u> ruins

   E All correct

42 **F** hard to <u>swallow</u>

   G happy <u>occasion</u>

   H <u>locate</u> the station

   J <u>usuelly</u> right

   K All correct

43 **A** <u>important</u> meeting

   B <u>diffrent</u> route

   C <u>among</u> the best

   D <u>autumn</u> leaves

   E All correct

44 **F** three <u>quarts</u>   **J** two <u>teaspoons</u>

   G one <u>acre</u>   **K** All correct

   H ten <u>minites</u>

GO

Name _____

Directions: Read the paragraph that tells about a challenging experience that one student had.

      I've never been as scared as I was the first time I tried to go inline skating. My legs felt like jelly. The skates kept slipping out from under me. I'd thought I'd just soar through the air in jumps and spins, but I found out that skating isn't as easy as it looks. Since then, I've been practicing, and I'm getting better. With even more practice, I know that I'll continue to improve.

Directions: Now, think about a challenging experience you have had. Write one or two sentences to answer each question below, and then use your answers to write a paragraph of your own.

What is a challenging experience you have faced?

_____

_____

_____

Why was the experience challenging? How did you feel when you first tried it?

_____

_____

_____

_____

Write your own paragraph on the lines below.

_____

_____

_____

_____

_____ **STOP**

Name _____

Mathematics

Lesson 1 Computation

 SAMPLE A

413
+ 133

A 320

B 446

C 546

D 556

E None of these

SAMPLE B

55 – 19 =

F 34

G 44

H 46

J 74

K None of these

 TIPS Skim the problems and do the easiest ones first. Check your answer by the opposite operation.

1

7291
+ 296

A 7005

B 6587

C 7585

D 7587

E None of these

3

3106
× 3

A 3109

B 9418

C 9318

D 9609

E None of these

2

4008
– 2021

F 2027

G 1987

H 2987

J 6029

K None of these

4

$\frac{1}{3} + \frac{1}{3} =$

F 0

G $\frac{1}{6}$

H $\frac{11}{13}$

J $\frac{1}{8}$

K None of these

STOP

Name _____

Lesson 2 Mathematics Skills

 What is the area of the shaded figure?

   A   5 square units

   B $5\frac{1}{2}$ square units

   C   6 square units

   D $6\frac{1}{2}$ square units

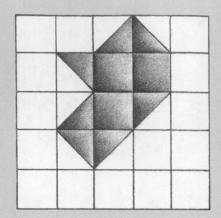

= 1 square unit

Think about what you are supposed to do before you start working.

Eliminate answers you know are wrong.

Before you mark your answer, compare it with the question. Does your answer make sense?

GO

Name _____

Our Hockey Team

5 Carla has 6 hockey cards. Ed and Carla together have 16 hockey cards. Judith and Ed together have 25 hockey cards. How many hockey cards does Judith have?

A 6

B 9

C 15

D 20

6 The table shows the number of goals Luke, Jacques, Pierre, and Roland have scored during the hockey season. If the trend continues, which player is most likely to score a goal in the next game?

Players	Luke	Jacques	Pierre	Roland
Number of Goals	///// /	///// ///// ////	///// ///	///

F Luke

G Jacques

H Pierre

J Roland

7 The number of people watching a hockey game is 900 when rounded to the nearest hundred and 850 when rounded to the nearest ten. Which of these could be the number of people watching the game?

A 847

B 849

C 856

D 852

GO

Name _____

8 After the hockey game, each of these players bought a can of soda from a machine that takes both coins and bills.

Soda
70¢

– Luke used only dimes.

– Jacques used only quarters.

– Pierre used only half-dollars.

– Roland used a dollar bill.

Which two players got the same amount of change?

F Luke and Jacques

G Jacques and Pierre

H Pierre and Roland

J Roland and Luke

9 The Card Shop receives a shipment of trading cards each month. There are 8 hockey cards in a pack, 12 packs in a box, and 16 boxes in a shipping crate. Which is the total number of hockey cards in the shipping crate?

A 1536

B 672

C 1436

D 662

8 cards
in a pack

12 packs
in a box

16 boxes
in a crate

GO

Name _____

Hair Color

Directions: The tally chart shows the hair color of some 5th-grade students. Study the chart. Then do numbers 10–12.

10 **Which of these questions could you answer using the information on the tally chart?**

   F How often do the students get their hair cut?

   G How many students dye their hair?

   H Which students have long hair?

   J How many more brown-haired students are there than blond-haired students?

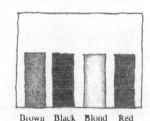

11 **Which graph below shows the data on the tally chart?**

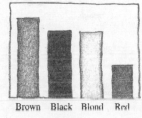
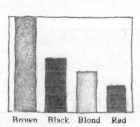
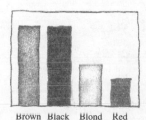

  A   **B**   **C**   **D**

12 **Which circle shows the fraction of the students on the tally chart that have black hair?**

  F   **G**   **H**   **J**

GO

Name _____

13 Lori's class used hobby sticks to make skeletons of solid figures. Study the picture of the prism and its skeleton.

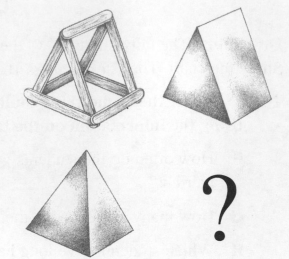

How many hobby sticks would be needed to make a skeleton of a rectangular pyramid?

A 9

B 8

C 7

D 4

14 How many pairs of congruent figures are on the grid?

F 4

G 5

H 6

J 7

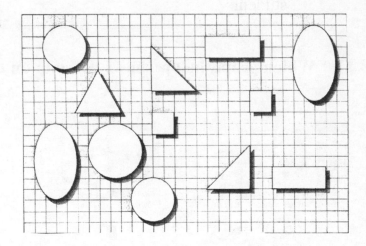

15 If = 1, then which of these pictures represents $1\frac{3}{8}$?

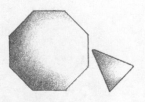

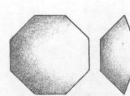

A   **B**   **C**   **D**

 GO

Test Prep

Name _____

16   1.14
       + 4.53

- **F** 5.57
- **G** 5.66
- **H** 5.76
- **J** 5.77
- **K** None of these

17 $20\frac{7}{8}$
        $- 5\frac{3}{8}$

- **A** $25\frac{1}{2}$
- **B** $15\frac{1}{2}$
- **C** $14\frac{1}{2}$
- **D** $15\frac{2}{7}$
- **E** None of these

18   3000
        × 42

- **F** 126,000
- **G** 120,420
- **H** 300,420
- **J** 300,042
- **K** None of these

19 $31\overline{)1085}$

- **A** 34
- **B** 34 R1
- **C** 35
- **D** 35 R1
- **E** None of these

20 $\frac{5}{6} - \frac{2}{3} =$

- **F** $\frac{1}{3}$
- **G** $1\frac{1}{9}$
- **H** $\frac{1}{6}$
- **J** 1
- **K** None of these

21   490 ÷ 7 =

- **A** 70
- **B** 90
- **C** 420
- **D** 560
- **E** None of these

STOP

Name _____

Lesson 3 Review

 SAMPLE D The numbers in each triangle are related according to a certain rule. Which of these is the missing top of the triangle?

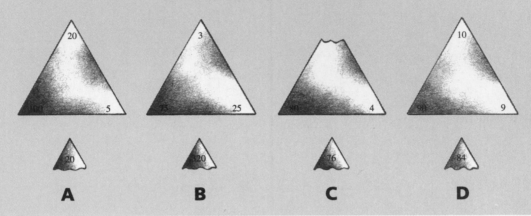

A   **B**   **C**   **D**

Directions: For numbers 22–25, you do not need to find exact answers. Use estimation to choose the best answer.

22 Jay took a test that had a true/false section, a matching section, and a multiple choice section. Look at the score card below. Which of these is the best estimate of his point total on the multiple choice section?

A 20 points

B 30 points

C 40 points

D 50 points

True/False	1–10
1 Wrong	
Matching	1–15
2 Wrong	
Multiple Choice	1–25
5 Wrong	
2 pts. per question.	

23 5700 ÷ 7

The answer to this problem is about

F 8000   **H** 80

G 800   **J** 8

24 Which of these is the best estimate of 57.4 + 79.7?

A less than 100

B between 100 and 150

C between 150 and 200

D greater than 200

25 Sharon earned $125.50 baby-sitting on weekend nights. She had $46.89 left after she bought some new clothes. Which of these is the best estimate of the cost of her clothes?

F $20.00   **H** $60.00

G $40.00   **J** $80.00

GO

Name _____

Our Favorite Subjects

Directions: The 5th graders at Memorial School voted for their favorite subject in school. They made a graph to show how they voted.

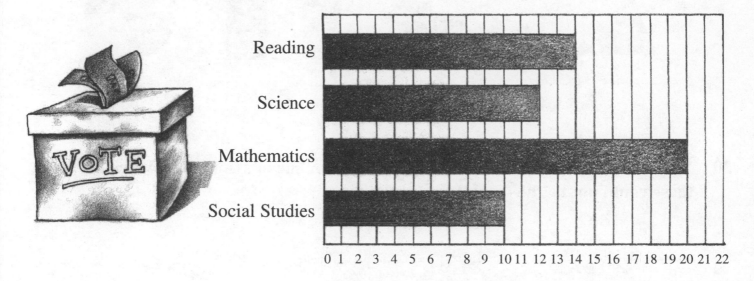

26 **How many more students voted for mathematics than voted for science?**

A 2   **C** 6

B 4   **D** 8

27 **Which of these could not happen if 8 more 5th graders added their votes to the graph?**

F Social studies could have the most votes.

G Science and math could have the same number of votes.

H Science could have more votes than reading.

J Social studies could have more votes than science.

28 **Which of these statements about the vote is true?**

A More than three-quarters of the 5th graders voted for mathematics.

B Exactly one-quarter of the 5th graders voted for reading.

C More than one-quarter of the 5th graders voted for social studies.

D Exactly one-quarter of the 5th graders voted for science.

GO

Name _____

29 **Which shape is exactly two-thirds shaded?**

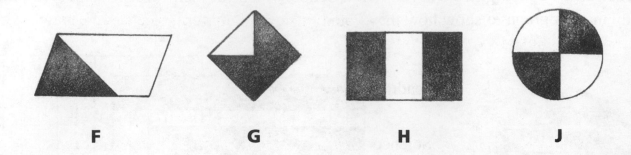

F   G   H   J

30 **Xavier cut an eight-sided piece of paper along a line of symmetry. Which of these could not be the result?**

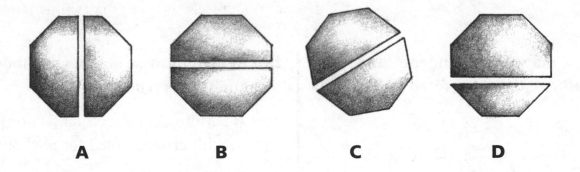

A   B   C   D

31 **Which of these points shows about where 3 × 87 would be put on the number line?**

F Point A

G Point B

H Point C

J Point D

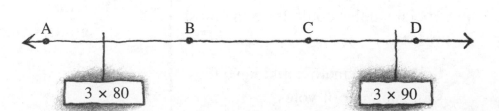

STOP

Test Prep

Name _____

Final Test Answer Sheet

Fill in **only one** letter for each item. If you change an answer, make sure to erase your first mark completely.

Unit 1: Reading, pages 53–58

A Ⓐ Ⓑ Ⓒ Ⓓ	**6** Ⓕ Ⓖ Ⓗ Ⓙ	**12** Ⓕ Ⓖ Ⓗ Ⓙ	**18** Ⓕ Ⓖ Ⓗ Ⓙ	**24** Ⓐ Ⓑ Ⓒ Ⓓ
1 Ⓐ Ⓑ Ⓒ Ⓓ	**7** Ⓐ Ⓑ Ⓒ Ⓓ	**13** Ⓐ Ⓑ Ⓒ Ⓓ	**19** Ⓕ Ⓖ Ⓗ Ⓙ	**25** Ⓐ Ⓑ Ⓒ Ⓓ
2 Ⓕ Ⓖ Ⓗ Ⓙ	**8** Ⓕ Ⓖ Ⓗ Ⓙ	**14** Ⓕ Ⓖ Ⓗ Ⓙ	**20** Ⓕ Ⓖ Ⓗ Ⓙ	
3 Ⓐ Ⓑ Ⓒ Ⓓ	**9** Ⓐ Ⓑ Ⓒ Ⓓ	**15** Ⓐ Ⓑ Ⓒ Ⓓ	**21** Ⓕ Ⓖ Ⓗ Ⓙ	
4 Ⓕ Ⓖ Ⓗ Ⓙ	**10** Ⓕ Ⓖ Ⓗ Ⓙ	**16** Ⓕ Ⓖ Ⓗ Ⓙ	**22** Ⓐ Ⓑ Ⓒ Ⓓ	
5 Ⓐ Ⓑ Ⓒ Ⓓ	**11** Ⓐ Ⓑ Ⓒ Ⓓ	**17** Ⓐ Ⓑ Ⓒ Ⓓ	**23** Ⓐ Ⓑ Ⓒ Ⓓ	

Unit 2: Language Arts, pages 59–67

A Ⓐ Ⓑ Ⓒ Ⓓ	**10** Ⓕ Ⓖ Ⓗ Ⓙ	**21** Ⓐ Ⓑ Ⓒ Ⓓ	**32** Ⓕ Ⓖ Ⓗ Ⓙ
1 Ⓐ Ⓑ Ⓒ Ⓓ	**11** Ⓐ Ⓑ Ⓒ Ⓓ	**22** Ⓕ Ⓖ Ⓗ Ⓙ	**33** Ⓐ Ⓑ Ⓒ Ⓓ
B Ⓐ Ⓑ Ⓒ Ⓓ	**12** Ⓕ Ⓖ Ⓗ Ⓙ	**23** Ⓐ Ⓑ Ⓒ Ⓓ	**34** Ⓕ Ⓖ Ⓗ Ⓙ
2 Ⓕ Ⓖ Ⓗ Ⓙ	**13** Ⓐ Ⓑ Ⓒ Ⓓ	**24** Ⓕ Ⓖ Ⓗ Ⓙ	**35** Ⓐ Ⓑ Ⓒ Ⓓ
3 Ⓐ Ⓑ Ⓒ Ⓓ	**14** Ⓕ Ⓖ Ⓗ Ⓙ	**25** Ⓐ Ⓑ Ⓒ Ⓓ	**36** Ⓕ Ⓖ Ⓗ Ⓙ
4 Ⓕ Ⓖ Ⓗ Ⓙ	**15** Ⓐ Ⓑ Ⓒ Ⓓ	**26** Ⓕ Ⓖ Ⓗ Ⓙ	**37** Ⓐ Ⓑ Ⓒ Ⓓ
5 Ⓐ Ⓑ Ⓒ Ⓓ	**16** Ⓕ Ⓖ Ⓗ Ⓙ Ⓚ	**27** Ⓐ Ⓑ Ⓒ Ⓓ	**38** Ⓕ Ⓖ Ⓗ Ⓙ
6 Ⓕ Ⓖ Ⓗ Ⓙ	**17** Ⓐ Ⓑ Ⓒ Ⓓ Ⓔ	**28** Ⓕ Ⓖ Ⓗ Ⓙ	**39** Ⓐ Ⓑ Ⓒ Ⓓ
7 Ⓐ Ⓑ Ⓒ Ⓓ	**18** Ⓕ Ⓖ Ⓗ Ⓙ Ⓚ	**29** Ⓐ Ⓑ Ⓒ Ⓓ	
8 Ⓕ Ⓖ Ⓗ Ⓙ	**19** Ⓐ Ⓑ Ⓒ Ⓓ Ⓔ	**30** Ⓕ Ⓖ Ⓗ Ⓙ	
9 Ⓐ Ⓑ Ⓒ Ⓓ	**20** Ⓕ Ⓖ Ⓗ Ⓙ	**31** Ⓐ Ⓑ Ⓒ Ⓓ	

Name _____

Final Test Answer Sheet

Unit 3: Mathematics, pages 68–76

A Ⓐ Ⓑ Ⓒ Ⓓ   10 Ⓕ Ⓖ Ⓗ Ⓙ   22 Ⓕ Ⓖ Ⓗ Ⓙ   34 Ⓕ Ⓖ Ⓗ Ⓙ

B Ⓕ Ⓖ Ⓗ Ⓙ Ⓚ   11 Ⓐ Ⓑ Ⓒ Ⓓ   23 Ⓐ Ⓑ Ⓒ Ⓓ   35 Ⓐ Ⓑ Ⓒ Ⓓ

1 Ⓐ Ⓑ Ⓒ Ⓓ Ⓔ   12 Ⓕ Ⓖ Ⓗ Ⓙ   24 Ⓕ Ⓖ Ⓗ Ⓙ   36 Ⓕ Ⓖ Ⓗ Ⓙ

2 Ⓕ Ⓖ Ⓗ Ⓙ Ⓚ   13 Ⓐ Ⓑ Ⓒ Ⓓ   25 Ⓐ Ⓑ Ⓒ Ⓓ   37 Ⓐ Ⓑ Ⓒ Ⓓ

3 Ⓐ Ⓑ Ⓒ Ⓓ Ⓔ   14 Ⓕ Ⓖ Ⓗ Ⓙ   26 Ⓕ Ⓖ Ⓗ Ⓙ   38 Ⓕ Ⓖ Ⓗ Ⓙ

4 Ⓕ Ⓖ Ⓗ Ⓙ Ⓚ   15 Ⓐ Ⓑ Ⓒ Ⓓ   27 Ⓐ Ⓑ Ⓒ Ⓓ   39 Ⓐ Ⓑ Ⓒ Ⓓ

5 Ⓐ Ⓑ Ⓒ Ⓓ Ⓔ   16 Ⓕ Ⓖ Ⓗ Ⓙ   28 Ⓕ Ⓖ Ⓗ Ⓙ   40 Ⓕ Ⓖ Ⓗ Ⓙ

6 Ⓕ Ⓖ Ⓗ Ⓙ Ⓚ   17 Ⓐ Ⓑ Ⓒ Ⓓ   29 Ⓐ Ⓑ Ⓒ Ⓓ   41 Ⓐ Ⓑ Ⓒ Ⓓ

C Ⓐ Ⓑ Ⓒ Ⓓ   18 Ⓕ Ⓖ Ⓗ Ⓙ   30 Ⓕ Ⓖ Ⓗ Ⓙ   42 Ⓕ Ⓖ Ⓗ Ⓙ

7 Ⓐ Ⓑ Ⓒ Ⓓ   19 Ⓐ Ⓑ Ⓒ Ⓓ   31 Ⓐ Ⓑ Ⓒ Ⓓ   43 Ⓐ Ⓑ Ⓒ Ⓓ

8 Ⓕ Ⓖ Ⓗ Ⓙ   20 Ⓕ Ⓖ Ⓗ Ⓙ   32 Ⓕ Ⓖ Ⓗ Ⓙ

9 Ⓐ Ⓑ Ⓒ Ⓓ   21 Ⓐ Ⓑ Ⓒ Ⓓ   33 Ⓐ Ⓑ Ⓒ Ⓓ

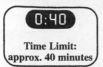

Time Limit: approx. 40 minutes

Name _____

Reading

Directions: Read the paragraph, then answer the question.

SAMPLE A

John practiced playing piano every day after school. Sometimes it wasn't easy, especially on days when the other kids were playing sports. He enjoyed sports, especially basketball, but he loved piano even more.

On a rainy Saturday, John would probably

A play basketball.

C play piano.

B watch basketball on television.

D play another musical instrument.

Directions: When Kiki and her family were shipwrecked on an island, they began a new life. Read the story about Kiki's home, then do numbers 1–9.

Survivors

As far as Kiki was concerned, the island had always been her home, and she loved it. She had been just about a year old when the ship she and her family had been on was caught in a great storm. She didn't remember their home in England, where she had been born, or boarding the sailing ship for Australia. Kiki certainly didn't remember how her family and a few dozen others had arrived on the island in lifeboats, or even how they had built houses and made new lives. Kiki's first memory was sitting in the warm lagoon with her mother's arms around her. Her brother and sister were splashing in the waves, and her father was in a small boat spearing fish.

The Martin family and the others who had survived the shipwreck had worked hard to make the island livable. Now, ten years after the disaster, the island was a wonderful place to grow up. Everyone had a comfortable home with furniture made out of wood, palm leaves, and vines. Their food came from the sea, from jungle plants, or from small gardens the survivors had planted. They were able to accomplish so much because chests of seeds, tools, and food had washed up on the beach in the weeks following the wreck. These chests gave the survivors a chance to build a new life on the island.

GO

Name _____

Kiki and the other children went to school just like other children, with the grownups taking turns teaching the children. They learned to write on large leaves using burnt sticks and to read from books that had been in several of the chests. They also learned arithmetic, science, history, and geography. But most of all, they learned about their island. Part of every school day was spent exploring the island and discovering more and more about its plants, animals, and geography.

It was on one of these outings to explore the island that Kiki and her friends saw the great ships. They had climbed to the highest peak on the island to learn about the sea birds that nested on the cliffs below. When the children reached the top of the peak, they spent a few minutes looking at the ocean all around them. Kiki spotted the four ships first, with their huge sails billowing in the wind. She shouted to her teacher, and soon everyone saw them. The ships were clearly headed toward the island.

By the time Kiki and her friends climbed down the mountain, the ships had reached the island, and the captain and crew were surprised to find other English settlers there. They had known about the shipwreck, of course, but had no idea there were survivors. The ships were heading to Australia, and the survivors were welcomed to join the crew on board.

That, however, was the problem. Almost all the survivors didn't want to leave the island, especially the children like Kiki who had spent most of their lives there or the dozen who had been born there. For them, the island was their world, and they couldn't imagine leaving it.

GO

1 This story is mostly about

   A a family leaving England for Australia.

   B survivors being rescued years later.

   C how people lived after a shipwreck.

   D children discovering sailing ships.

2 Which of these best describes Kiki's feelings at the end of the story?

   F She was frightened by the great ships.

   G She loved the island and didn't want to leave.

   H She wanted to finish the journey to Australia.

   J She was grateful for being rescued.

3 Which ideas from the story support your answer to number 2?

   A The children couldn't imagine leaving the island.

   B Kiki saw the great ships from a mountain top.

   C The survivors were welcomed to board the ship.

   D They had survived a terrible storm.

4 Which of these actions led to Kiki's spotting the ships?

   F splashing in the lagoon

   G spearing fish in the lagoon

   H climbing the mountain

   J looking for wood and palm leaves

5 The survivors were able to make the island a good place to live because they

   A were skilled at building things from wood.

   B found the chests with seeds, tools, and food.

   C decided not to continue to Australia.

   D believed that they would be rescued some day.

6 Imagine that the children were given a chance to vote on whether to leave the island or stay. Which of these would probably happen?

   F Most would vote to stay.

   G Most would vote to go.

   H It would be a tie vote.

   J They would not want to vote.

GO

7 In the year after the shipwreck, the feelings of the survivors probably changed from

A fear to anger.

B boredom to tolerance.

C joy to confusion.

D sadness to acceptance.

8 The story states that, "It was on one of these outings to explore the island" that the ships were seen. Used in this way, the word *outings* probably means

F a brief voyage.

G a walking trip.

H an open field.

J an empty cave.

9 Here is a time line of what happens in the passage.

Families board ship	Storm wrecks ship	Chests are found	?	New ships appear

Which of these events should go in the empty box?

A Kiki grows up

B Settlers reach America

C Kiki is born

D Settlers leave England

GO

Name _____

Directions: Read the passage. Then answer the questions.

There are many differences between frogs and toads. Frogs have narrow bodies and ridges down their backs. They have large, round ear membranes and small teeth in their upper jaws. Their long hind legs **enable** them to take long leaps. They have smooth, moist, soft skin. Most frogs are water-dwellers. They lay clumps of eggs in their watery habitat.

In contrast, toads have chubby bodies and ridges on their heads. Toads make their homes on land and their skin is thick, dry, and bumpy. A toad's short legs **limit** it to short leaps only. Their ear membranes are smaller than frogs'. They have no teeth. Although toads are land-dwellers, they deposit their eggs in water as frogs do. However, they lay eggs in strings rather than clumps.

10 **What would be a good title for this passage?**

F "Laying Eggs in Water"

G "Frogs and Toads: What's the Difference?"

H "Amphibians"

J "Similarities Between Frogs and Toads"

11 **In this passage, the word *limit* means**

A to restrict or hold back.

B boundary.

C the greatest number or amount allowed.

D restriction.

12 **Which word is an antonym for *enable*?**

F prevent

G assist

H inedible

J teach

13 **Which of the following is not a fact?**

A Toads have chubbier bodies than frogs.

B Frogs have longer hind legs than toads.

C Toads have smaller ear membranes than frogs.

D Frogs are more attractive than toads.

GO

Name _____

Directions: Choose the best answer for each of the following. Mark the letter of your choice for each next to the correct number on your answer sheet.

14 **Raise** is to **uplift** as **bring down** is to _____.

   F depress   **H** pull

   G undo   **J** rely

16 **Email** is to **write** as **telephone** is to _____.

   F speak   **H** ring

   G listen   **J** download

15 **Millimeter** is to **meter** as **gram** is to _____.

   A liter

   B kilometer

   C kilogram

   D milligram

17 **Biographer** is to **life story** as **reporter** is to _____.

   A science fiction

   B personal narrative

   C newspaper

   D newspaper article

Directions: Match words with the same meanings.

18 **silence**   **F** berate

19 **belittle**   **G** amusement

20 **questionable**   **H** quiet

21 **entertainment**   **J** unreliable

Directions: Match words with the opposite meanings.

22 **create**   **A** darken

23 **illuminate**   **B** repulse

24 **impress**   **C** destroy

25 **deny**   **D** admit

STOP

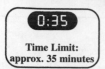

0:35

Time Limit:
approx. 35 minutes

Name _____

Language Arts

Directions: For Sample A and number 1, read the sentences. Choose the word that correctly completes **both** sentences.

Directions: For Sample B and numbers 2 and 3, choose the word that means the **opposite** of the underlined word.

SAMPLE A We can _____ at the park.
I'll see you at the track _____.

    A play   **C** relax

    B competition   **D** meet

SAMPLE B <u>spoiled</u> fruit.

    A fresh

    B rotten

    C moldy

    D dirty

1 This _____ of books is heavy.
The book is about an unsolved _____.

    A box   **C** case

    B crime   **D** bag

2 <u>smile</u> at her

    F frown   **H** whisper

    G yell   **J** wink

3 <u>expected</u> result

    A anticipated   **C** disappointing

    B surprising   **D** pleasing

Directions: For numbers 4 and 5, read the paragraph. For each numbered blank, there is a list of words with the same number. Choose the word from each list that best completes the meaning of the paragraph.

For many years, jigsaw puzzles have entertained both children and adults. In recent years, puzzles have become even more __(4)__ and enjoyable. Now there are three-dimensional puzzles that look exactly like the things they __(5)__. For example, you can find 3-D puzzles that represent castles, famous buildings, and even a camera. Amazingly, the camera can even take pictures.

4   **F** boring   **H** simple

      G inexpensive   **J** challenging

5   **A** imitate   **C** improve

      B replace   **D** assemble

GO

Name _____

Directions: For numbers 6 and 7, choose the answer that is written correctly and shows the correct capitalization and punctuation.

6 **F** You know that I don't like carrots Aunt Latifa.

    G Have you ever made carrot salad, Inez?

    H Dad! do I have to finish my carrots?

    J Molly can you remember to water the carrots tomorrow?

7 **A** Rain is good for plants and, it provides water for people.

    B When it rains, the sky gets dark; and the temperature drops.

    C The sound of rain is usually quiet, but, during a storm it can be loud.

    D The rain fell steadily, and the fields began to flood.

Directions: For numbers 8–11, look at the underlined part of the paragraph. Choose the answer that shows the best capitalization and punctuation for that part.

(8)   Leo wrote an article called <u>"lizards"</u> for the school paper.

(9)   He <u>didn't</u> expect anyone to get excited about it, but they did.

(10)   His teacher <u>was. Pleased</u> that Leo had done such a good job.

(11)   "This was the best story you ever <u>wrote she</u> said.

8 **F** lizards

    G "Lizards"

    H lizards.

    J Correct as it is

10 **F** was? Pleased

    G was pleased.

    H was pleased

    J Correct as it is

9 **A** didnt

    B didnt'

    C did'nt

    D Correct as it is

11 **A** wrote," she

    B wrote she,"

    C wrote." She

    D Correct as it is

GO

Name _____

Directions: For numbers 12–15, choose the word that is spelled correctly and best completes the sentence.

12 **I'll be there in a _____.**

    F minit

    G minite

    H minnute

    J minute

13 **Marsha will meet us _____.**

    A afterward

    B afterword

    C afterwerd

    D aftirward

14 **What a _____ mistake we made!**

    F terible   **H** terrible

    G terribull   **J** terrable

15 **My birthday is on the _____.**

    A twelth   **C** twelfeth

    B twelveth   **D** twelfth

Directions: For numbers 16–19, read each phrase. Find the underlined word that is *not* spelled correctly. If all the underlined words are spelled correctly, mark "All correct."

16 **F** <u>division</u> problem

    G be <u>pateint</u>

    H <u>brightly</u> colored

    J was <u>frightened</u>

    K All correct

17 **A** small <u>apartment</u>

    B <u>heavier</u> package

    C <u>special</u> place

    D next <u>century</u>

    E All correct

18 **F** <u>cuccumber</u> seeds

    G <u>pursue</u> her dream

    H <u>reference</u> section

    J <u>political</u> <u>campaign</u>

    K All correct

19 **A** <u>ceiling</u> fan   **D** <u>eighth</u> in line

    B <u>chief</u> of police   **E** All correct

    C <u>niether</u> of them

GO

Name _____

Directions: For numbers 20–25, mark the letter of the punctuation mark that is needed to complete each sentence correctly.

20 "Mark and Alex where are you going?" asked Mrs. Anderson.

;	,	.	none
F	G	H	J

21 Please add these items to our shopping list bread, milk, orange juice, lettuce, apples, and eggs.

:	,	!	none
A	B	C	D

22 We listened to the Presidents inaugural address in class today.

,	.	'	none
F	G	H	J

23 "What an incredible sight this is" exclaimed one of the tourists.

?	!	,	none
A	B	C	D

24 Maria plays the French horn and cello; Lisa plays piano, flute, and piccolo.

,	:	.	none
F	G	H	J

25 "Unless you combine and mix the ingredients thoroughly, warned Mom, "the batter will be lumpy."

"	'	,	none
A	B	C	D

GO

Directions: For numbers 26–29, mark the letter of the sentence that is written correctly and shows the correct punctuation and capitalization.

26 **F** Pittsburgh, Pennsylvania the "Steel City," has over 700 bridges.

    G The allegheny and the monongahela, two rivers bordering downtown Pittsburgh, join to form the ohio river.

    H In 1758, General John Forbes built a fort near the fork of the two rivers and named it Fort Pitt in honor of the prime minister of Great Britain.

    J Soon after, british settlers began to build a community outside the fort which Forbes named Pittsburgh.

27 **A** Did you know that the Grand Coulee dam, on the Columbia River, is the largest concrete dam in the world?

    B Mrs James our social studies teacher showed us photos of the dam and all the other neat places she visited on her trip to Washington.

    C I didn't realize that mount Ranier was actually a volcano like mount st Helens!

    D I'd really like to visit the space needle and ride the monorail in Seattle Washington.

28 **F** The travel brochures for Arizona and New Mexico are on Dads desk?

    G Lets look up some of these places online before we decide.

    H Don't you think it would be fantastic to visit the grand canyon, the painted desert, and the petrified forest?

    J Well, Mom and Dad want to see New Mexico's Carlsbad Caverns.

29 **A** "Mrs. Wilson and I," Began Mr. Wilson, our neighbor, have visited all 50 states."

    B "Which state did you like the most, Mr. Wilson," asked Adam?

    C "That's really a hard question to answer," he said, "because every state has so many interesting things to see and do."

    D "We're going to Maine in august, said Adam, so maybe you can show us some of your videos."

GO

Name _____

Directions: For numbers 30–35, mark the letter of the word or words that correctly complete each sentence.

30 **Mai's brother walks _____ than she does.**

   F rapider

   G more rapidly

   H rapidlier

   J more rapid

31 **My brother and I taught _____ to swim.**

   A himself

   B myself

   C themselves

   D ourselves

32 **Tom misses school _____.**

   F real infrequently

   G really infrequent

   H really infrequently

   J real infrequent

33 **_____ are very good friends.**

   A He, she, and I

   B He, she, and me

   C Him, her, and I

   D He, she, and me

34 **Which one of _____ shirts do you prefer?**

   F them

   G these

   H this

   J that

35 **We have to replace the sidewalk _____ the weather turns too cold.**

   A while

   B until

   C before

   D after

GO

Directions: For numbers 36–39, mark the letter of the sentence that is correctly written.

36 **F** She don't have nothing to do.

   G You can't tell nobody nothing about this.

   H He doesn't have anything more to say.

   J Nobody wants none of that salad.

37 **A** Ann and I was walking in the woods yesterday.

   B I am picking berries when I noticed the poison ivy.

   C Now my arms and legs are covered with blisters.

   D These pills and this cream is supposed to stop the itching.

38 **F** I felt worst today than I did yesterday.

   G I hope I feel more better soon.

   H The doctor says it could get worser tomorrow.

   J I have never felt so sick before.

39 **A** Kwanzaa is an African-American holiday based on an African festival.

   B The festival beginning on December 26 and lasting seven days.

   C Comes from the Swahili phrases *matunda ya kwanza* meaning *first fruits*.

   D In 1966 in the United States by M. Ron Karenga, a professor.

STOP

Name _____

Directions: Read the paragraph below about what one student does to help at home. Then think of one thing you do to help at home. Write a paragraph that explains how to do it. Use words such as *first, next, then, finally,* and *last.*

    I help out at home by doing the wash. First, I separate clothes to be washed in cold water and in hot water. Next, I put the clothes into the water. Then I add detergent. When the clothes are clean, I put them into the dryer. Finally, I hang them up or fold them. This chore is a big contribution to my family, and I get to put away my own clothes exactly the way I like them!

_____

_____

_____

_____

_____

_____

_____

_____

_____

_____

_____

_____

_____

_____

_____

GO

Name _____

Directions: Read the paragraph below that compares two kinds of vacations. Then think of two other things to compare and contrast, such as different sports, musicians, or books. Use your ideas to write a paragraph. As you write, use words such as *same, like, different, unlike, but,* and *however.*

    A beach vacation and a ski vacation are alike in some ways and different in others. On both kinds of vacations, people can relax and spend time with friends and family. However, some people prefer the beach, because, unlike the ski slopes, the beach is usually warm. Other people find skiing much more exciting than sitting in a beach chair and splashing in the waves. Whether it is a beach vacation or a ski vacation, it all comes down to what you like to do more.

_____

_____

_____

_____

_____

_____

_____

_____

_____

_____

_____

_____

_____

STOP

Name _____

Mathematics

SAMPLE A

469
+ 225

A 244

B 684

C 694

D 695

E None of these

SAMPLE B

87.8
− 72.4

F 5.4

G 14.5

H 16.2

J 15.4

K None of these

1

23
× 32

A 736

B 636

C 55

D 115

E None of these

4 $5\frac{7}{8} - 2\frac{3}{8} =$

F $2\frac{1}{2}$

G $3\frac{3}{4}$

H $3\frac{3}{8}$

J $3\frac{1}{2}$

K None of these

2 $6.00 − $0.35

F $6.35

G $5.65

H $5.75

J $5.35

K None of these

5 $510 \times 38 =$

A 19,380

B 548

C 51,038

D 18,390

E None of these

3 18⟌90

A 5

B 4

C 4 R2

D 5 R4

E None of these

6

89.7
+ 25.6

F 114.3

G 64.3

H 105.3

J 104.3

K None of these

GO

Name _____

C

Points M and N represent certain numbers on the number line. Which of these problems would give an answer of about 10?

A N + M

B N − M

C N × M

D N ÷ M

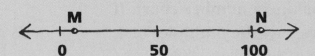

---

7 Parallelogram QRST slid to a new position on the grid as shown. Which moves describe the slide?

A 1 right, 4 down

B 1 right, 5 down

C 2 right, 4 down

D 1 right, 3 down

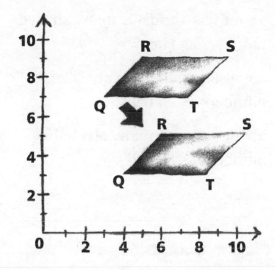

---

8 Study this pattern. If the pattern continues, how many stars will be in the fourth position?

F 14

G 16

H 18

J 20

Position		Number of Stars
1	★ ★ ★ ★	4
2	★ ★ ★ ★ ★ ★ ★ ★	8
3	★ ★ ★ ★ ★ ★ ★ ★ ★ ★ ★ ★	12
4		?

GO

Name _____

The Hundreds Hunt

Directions: Mr. Pontario's students are making number charts and labeling the squares from 1 to 100. Use Harry's number chart to do numbers 9 and 10.

9 **Liza is making a number chart. If she shades only the multiples of 4, her chart will have**

  A about three-fourths as many shaded numbers as Harry's.

  B about two-thirds as many shaded numbers as Harry's.

  C about one-half as many shaded numbers as Harry's.

  D about twice as many shaded numbers as Harry's.

HARRY'S CHART

1	2	3	4	5	6	7	8	9	10
11	12	13	14	15	16	17	18	19	20
21	22	23	24	25	26	27	28	29	30
31	32	33	34	35	36	37	38	39	40
41	42	43	44	45	46	47	48	49	50
51	52	53	54	55	56	57	58	59	60
61	62	63	64	65	66	67	68	69	70
71	72	73	74	75	76	77	78	79	80
81	82	83	84	85	86	87	88	89	90
91	92	93	94	95	96	97	98	99	100

10 **Tenisha just made a number chart on which she shaded all the multiples of 5. Which pattern shows the shading on her number chart?**

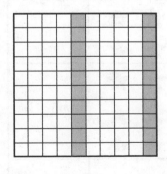
F

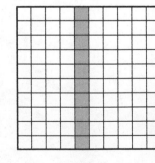
G

H

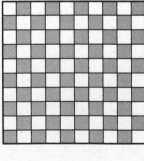
J

GO

Test Prep

11 Which of these number sentences could be used to find the cost of 6 dozen pens?

A $4.59 + 6 =

B $4.59 − 6 =

C $4.59 × 6 =

D $4.59 ÷ 6 =

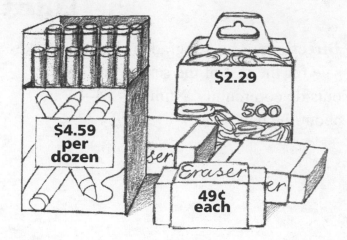

$2.29
500
$4.59
per
dozen
Eraser
49¢
each

12 Mrs. Lynch showed a container of jelly beans to her class. She said she would give it to the student who guessed the correct number of jelly beans inside it. The first four students guessed 352, 267, 195, and 454, respectively. What was the average of these four guesses?

F 300

G 317

H 320

J 323

13 If all these chips were put into a bag, what is the probability that you would pick a chip with a letter that comes before M in the alphabet?

A $\frac{3}{5}$

B $\frac{3}{8}$

C $\frac{5}{3}$

D $\frac{5}{8}$

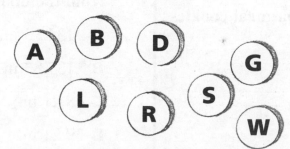

GO

Name _____

Bake Sale

Directions: The 5th grade is having a bake sale for the rest of the school and the outside community. Numbers 14–17 are about the bake sale.

14 There are 120 students in the fifth grade. Only 87 of these students contributed baked goods. How many students did not contribute baked goods?

F 87

G 207

H 43

J 33

15 The oatmeal cookies are small, so there are 3 cookies in each plastic bag. There are 45 bags of these cookies. How many oatmeal cookies are there in all?

A 48

B 120

C 135

D 15

16 The local bakery donated 112 blueberry muffins. There are 16 blueberries in each muffin. How many blueberries did the bakery use in all?

F 784   **H** 1782

G 128   **J** 1792

17 Thelma and Arnold collected the money. Thelma sat 71.52 inches from the exit door, and Arnold sat 63.31 inches farther from the exit door than Thelma sat. How far from the door did Arnold sit?

A 134.83 in.

B 135.83 in.

C 8.21 in.

D 9.21 in.

GO

Name _____

Directions: Find the correct answer to solve each problem.

18 **What number does CXVII represent?**

  F 62   **H** 117

  G 67   **J** 542

19 **What is the name of this figure?**

  A sphere

  B rectangular prism

  C triangular prism

  D cylinder

20 **What is 456,517 rounded to the nearest thousand?**

  F 460,000

  G 457,000

  H 454,000

  J 456,000

21 **Which of the following is a right triangle?**

  A

  B

  C

  D

22 **What letter represents point 4, 2?**

  F A

  G C

  H B

  J D

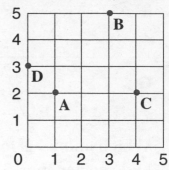

23 **What is the square root of 16?**

  A 256   **C** 4

  B 8   **D** 1

24 **Which figure shows intersecting lines, but not perpendicular lines?**

  F S

  G _____

  H X

  J

25 **What number has an 8 in the millions place and a 2 in the ten-thousands place?**

  A 8,912,703

  B 8,721,034

  C 8,241,037

  D 2,781,654

GO

26 What figure has vertical and horizontal symmetry?

F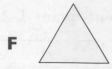

H

G

J

27 Which animal is longer than 156 inches and shorter than 216 inches?

A   African elephant

B   Hippopotamus

C   White rhinoceros

D   Giraffe

Animal	Length (in feet)	Weight (in pounds)
African Elephant	24	14,432
White Rhinoceros	14	7,937
Hippopotamus	13	5,512
Giraffe	19	2,257

28 What is the perimeter of this figure?

F   101 inches

G   98 inches

H   76 inches

J   38 inches

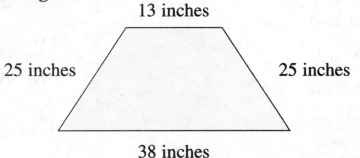

13 inches

25 inches   25 inches

38 inches

29 Which is the best estimate for the height of a room?

A   3 inches

B   3 feet

C   3 yards

D   3 miles

GO

Name _____

Directions: Find the correct answer to solve each problem.

30 **23,300 – 17,984 =**

F   5,316

G   5,326

H   6,626

J   41,284

31 **0.36** ☐ $\frac{3}{5}$

A   >

B   =

C   <

D   Not enough information

32 **78.576 + 412.82 =**

F   1,198.58

G   491.396

H   490.396

J   119.848

33 **1984 – 894.5 =**

A   986.5

B   1,089.5

C   1,189

D   2,879

34 **24,000 ÷ 60 =**

F   4,000

G   400

H   40

J   None of these

35 **765 + 456 + 835 + 490 =**

A   2,056

B   2,456

C   2,546

D   None of these

36 **Find the average for this set of numbers: 47, 83, 15, 22, 67.**

F   58.5   H   43.5

G   47   J   None of these

37 $\frac{1}{3} + 2\frac{1}{3} + \frac{4}{9} =$

A $3\frac{1}{9}$

B   3

C $2\frac{2}{3}$

D   None of these

GO

Name _____

Directions: Find the correct answer to solve each problem.

38 Five friends each had 36 prize tokens from the arcade. Two other friends each had 25 prize tokens. The 7 friends decided to combine their tokens and then divide them equally. How many tokens will each friend get?

F 8 tokens   **H** 32 tokens

G 25 tokens   **J** 33 tokens

39 James earned $15.85 each week for his chores. If James saves all of his money for 8 weeks, how much money will he have?

A $12.68

B $120.00

C $125.40

D $126.80

40 Luca finished his homework at 8:37 p.m. If he started his homework 92 minutes earlier, at what time did Luca begin his homework?

F 7:05 p.m.

G 7:09 p.m.

H 7:35 p.m.

J 11:09 p.m.

41 Martin made a bowl of punch using 14 gallons of juice. How many quarts of punch did Martin make?

A 112 quarts   **C** 28 quarts

B 56 quarts   **D** None of the above

42 Jaime read for 30 minutes on Monday, 47 minutes on Tuesday, 64 minutes on Wednesday, and 81 minutes on Thursday. Which statement describes Jaime's pattern for reading?

F Add 15 minutes each day

G Subtract 17 minutes each day

H Add 12 minutes each day

J Add 17 minutes each day

43 An aquarium has a collection of 148 fish. It is going to expand its collection to 500 fish. If 8 new fish are added each week, how long will it take to get to 500 fish?

A 15 weeks

B 19 weeks

C 43 weeks

D 44 weeks

STOP

Grade 5 Answer Key

Page 15
- **A.** C
- **B.** F

Page 17
- **1.** A

Page 18
- **2.** F
- **3.** B
- **4.** H
- **5.** A

Page 19
- **6.** J
- **7.** A
- **8.** J
- **9.** A
- **10.** G
- **11.** B

Page 20
- **12.** J
- **13.** A
- **14.** H

Page 22
- **15.** B
- **16.** F
- **17.** B
- **18.** H

Page 23
- **19.** B
- **20.** J
- **21.** B
- **22.** G

Page 24
- **C.** C

Page 25
- **23.** D

Page 26
- **24.** G
- **25.** D
- **26.** G
- **27.** A

Page 27
- **D.** B
- **28.** D
- **29.** G

Page 28
- **30.** D
- **31.** J

Page 29
- **32.** B
- **33.** F

Page 30
- **A.** B
- **1.** A
- **2.** J
- **B.** B
- **3.** D
- **4.** H

Page 31
- **5.** B
- **6.** F
- **7.** C
- **8.** G
- **9.** B
- **10.** G

Page 32
- **C.** D
- **11.** C
- **12.** G
- **13.** A
- **14.** J

Page 33
- **15.** D
- **16.** G
- **17.** B
- **18.** F
- **19.** A

Page 34
- **D.** A
- **20.** C
- **21.** F
- **22.** C
- **E.** E
- **23.** G
- **24.** E

Page 37
- **F.** A
- **25.** D
- **26.** F
- **27.** B
- **28.** H
- **29.** A
- **30.** G

Page 38
- **31.** C
- **32.** J
- **33.** A
- **34.** F
- **35.** C
- **36.** G

Page 39
- **37.** B
- **38.** F
- **39.** D
- **40.** J
- **41.** E
- **42.** J
- **43.** B
- **44.** H

Grade 5 Answer Key

Page 41
A. C
B. K
1. D
2. G
3. C
4. K

Page 42
C. D

Page 43
5. C
6. G
7. D

Page 44
8. H
9. A

Page 45
10. J
11. B
12. F

Page 46
13. B
14. G
15. D

Page 47
16. K
17. B
18. F
19. C
20. H
21. A

Page 48
D. A
22. C
23. G
24. B
25. J

Page 49
26. D
27. F
28. B

Page 50
29. H
30. D
31. H

Page 53
A. C

Page 55
1. C
2. G
3. A
4. H
5. B
6. F

Page 56
7. D
8. G
9. A

Page 57
10. G
11. A
12. F
13. D

Page 58
14. F
15. C
16. F
17. D
18. H
19. F
20. J
21. G
22. C
23. A
24. B
25. D

Page 59
A. D
1. C
B. A
2. F
3. B
4. J
5. A

Page 60
6. G
7. D
8. G
9. D
10. H
11. A

Page 61
12. J
13. A
14. H
15. D
16. G
17. E
18. F
19. C

Page 62
20. G
21. A
22. F
23. B
24. J
25. A

Page 63
26. H
27. A
28. J
29. C

Page 64
30. G
31. D
32. H
33. A
34. G
35. C

Grade 5 Answer Key

Page 65
36. H
37. C
38. J
39. A

Page 68
A. C
B. J
1. A
2. G
3. A
4. J
5. A
6. K

Page 69
C. B
7. A
8. G

Page 70
9. D
10. F

Page 71
11. C
12. G
13. D

Page 72
14. J
15. C
16. J
17. A

Page 73
18. H
19. C
20. G
21. D
22. G
23. C
24. H
25. B

Page 74
26. G
27. C
28. F
29. C

Page 75
30. F
31. C
32. G
33. B
34. G
35. C
36. J
37. A

Page 76
38. H
39. D
40. F
41. B
42. J
43. D

Grade 5 Answer Key

Page 35
Answers will vary, but should identify something specific that students have mixed feelings about, such as their neighborhood.

Answers will vary, but should include a specific example of something students do not like about their topic. Sample answer: I don't like all the traffic that travels through our neighborhood.

Answers will vary, but should include a specific example of something students like about their topic. Sample answer: I like the way our neighbors all get together outside on summer nights.

Paragraphs will vary, but should reflect the content of students' answers for the previous questions and include a topic sentence followed by detail sentences in logical order. See sample paragraph in writing prompt.

Page 36
Answers will vary, but should include a fictional character that could support a story. Students' reasoning should clearly identify some of the character's traits. Sample answer: I would write about Ling, a girl who always wants to win, but doesn't want to be a team player. She will be the main character because she has an important lesson to learn, and finding out how she learns this lesson will be interesting for the reader.

Answers will vary, but should include one or more settings. Sample answer: The story will take place now on playing fields at Ling's school and other schools nearby.

Answers will vary, but should include a clear problem and solution. More sophisticated answers might include a character's inner personal conflict, as well as the conflict happening externally within the story. Sample answer: José has a friend who needs to be a star in practice to make the team. This is his friend's dream. José decides to back away and stop taking all the attention to let his friend shine during the practice.

Stories will vary, but should reflect the content of students' answers for the previous questions and a clear sequence of events. See sample paragraph in writing prompt.

Page 40
Answers will vary, but should state a specific challenging experience, rather than a vague idea. Sample answer: I have learned to dive off the high board.

Answers will vary, but should clearly explain why the experience was challenging. Sample answer: This experience was challenging because the board was very high, and I had always been afraid of heights.

Paragraphs will vary, but should reflect the content of students' answers for the previous questions. See sample paragraph in writing prompt.

Page 66
Paragraphs will vary, but should tell how to do only one activity. Paragraphs should show knowledge of an informative how-to paragraph, including time-order words. The order of the steps should be logical. Topics might include: how to take care of the lawn or how to clean the kitchen thoroughly. See sample paragraph in writing prompt.

Page 67
Paragraphs will vary, but should compare and contrast at least two items clearly. Key words such as *same, like, different, unlike, but,* and *however* should be included. See sample paragraph in writing prompt.